Phillips Brooks

The Influence of Jesus

Delivered in the Church of the Holy Trinity in February, 1879

Phillips Brooks

The influence of Jesus
Delivered in the Church of the Holy Trinity in February, 1879

ISBN/EAN: 9783337284312

Printed in Europe, USA, Canada, Australia, Japan

Cover: Foto ©Lupo / pixelio.de

More available books at **www.hansebooks.com**

The Bohlen Lectures 1879

THE

Influence of Jesus

BY THE

Rt. Rev. PHILLIPS BROOKS, D.D.

Delivered in the Church of the Holy Trinity, Philadelphia, in February, 1879

NEW YORK
E. P. DUTTON & COMPANY
31 West Twenty-Third St.
1894

THE JOHN BOHLEN LECTURESHIP.

JOHN BOHLEN, who died in this city on the 26th day of April, 1874, bequeathed to trustees a fund of One Hundred Thousand Dollars, to be distributed to religious and charitable objects in accordance with the well-known wishes of the testator.

By a deed of trust, executed June 2, 1875, the trustees under the will of Mr. Bohlen transferred and paid over to "The Rector, Church Wardens, and Vestrymen of the Church of the Holy Trinity, Philadelphia," in trust, a sum of money for certain designated purposes, out of which fund the sum of Ten Thousand Dollars was set apart for the endowment of THE JOHN BOHLEN LECTURESHIP, upon the following terms and conditions:—

The money shall be invested in good substantial and safe securities, and held in trust for a fund to be called The John Bohlen Lectureship, and the income shall be applied annually to the payment of a qualified person, whether clergyman or layman, for the delivery and publication of at least one hundred copies of two or more lecture sermons. These Lectures shall be delivered at such time and place, in the city of Philadelphia, as the persons nominated to appoint the lecturer shall from time to time determine, giving at least six months notice to the person appointed to deliver the same, when the same may conveniently be done, and in no case selecting the same person as lecturer a second time within a period of five years. The payment shall be made to said lecturer, after the lectures have been printed and received by the trustees, of all the income for the year derived from said fund, after defraying the expense of printing the lectures and the other incidental expenses attending the same.

The subject of such lectures shall be such as is within the terms set forth in the will of the Rev. John Bampton, for the delivery of what are known as the "Bampton Lectures," at Oxford, or any other subject distinctively connected with or relating to the Christian Religion.

The lecturer shall be appointed annually in the month of May, or as soon thereafter as can conveniently be done, by the persons, who for the time being, shall hold the offices of Bishop of the Protestant Episcopal Church of the Diocese in which is the Church of the Holy Trinity; the Rector of said Church; the Professor of Biblical Learning, the Professor of Systematic Divinity, and the Professor of Ecclesiastical History, in the Divinity School of the Protestant Episcopal Church in Philadelphia.

In case either of said offices are vacant the others may nominate the lecturer.

Under this trust the Rev. PHILLIPS BROOKS, S.T.D., of Boston, was appointed to deliver the lectures for the year 1879.

PHILADELPHIA, Easter, 1879.

CONTENTS.

LECTURE I.
The Influence of Jesus on the Moral Life of Man . 9

LECTURE II.
The Influence of Jesus on the Social Life of Man . 71

LECTURE III.
The Influence of Jesus on the Emotional Life of Man 139

LECTURE IV.
The Influence of Jesus on the Intellectual Life of Man 207

I.

THE INFLUENCE OF JESUS
ON THE MORAL LIFE OF MAN.

THE INFLUENCE OF JESUS

ON THE MORAL LIFE OF MAN.

WHAT is the power of Christianity over man,—its source, its character, its issue? This is the question which I wish to study with you in these four lectures which I have been invited to deliver. But it is necessary at the outset that I should indicate the limits within which I wish to work. All that the subject, as I have stated it, would include, not four nor forty lectures could undertake to treat.

I have been led, then, to think of Christianity, and to speak of it, — at least in these lectures, — not as a system of doctrine, but as a personal force, behind which and in which there lies one great inspiring idea, which it is the work of the personal force to impress upon the life of man, with which the personal force is always struggling to fill mankind. The personal force is the nature of Jesus, full of humanity, full of divinity, and powerful with a love for man which combines in itself every element that enters into love of the completest kind. The inspiring idea is the fatherhood of God, and the childhood of every man to Him. Upon the race and upon the individual, Jesus is always bringing into more and more perfect revelation the certain truth that man, and every man, is the child of God. This is the sum of the work of the Incarnation. A hundred other statements regarding it, regarding Him who was incarnate, are true; but all statements concerning Him hold their truth within this truth, — that Jesus came to restore the fact of God's fatherhood to man's knowledge, and to its central place of power over man's life. Jesus is mysteriously the Word of God made flesh. He is the worker of amazing miracles upon the bodies and the souls of men. He is the convincer of sin. He is the Savior by suffering. But behind all these, as the purpose for which He is all these, He is the redeemer of man into the fatherhood of God. It would be deeply interesting to dwell on any one of these special aspects of His wondrous life; but when we want to gather into one great comprehensive statement the purpose for which Jesus lived, and the power which His life has had over the lives of men, we must seize His great idea and find His power there. For every man's power is his idea multiplied by and projected through his personality. The special actions which he does are only the points at which his power shows itself, — the tips of his powerful life, where its magnetic force is manifested, but not where it is created. And so the power of Jesus is the idea of Jesus multiplied and projected through the person of Jesus. His power is not in the miracles that He did, not even in the marvellous nature which He bore, but in the great truth, the primal and final fact of all the universe, so far as man has any part in it, which the whole nature of the Savior uttered, and with whose splendor every miraculous touch of that nature on the world, or on man's body or man's soul, burst forth into light.

I have said already what that idea is, — the relation of childhood and fatherhood between man and God. Man is the child of God by nature He is ignorant and rebellious, — the prodigal child of God ; but his ignorance and rebellion never break that first relationship. It is always a child ignorant of his Father ; always a child rebellious against his Father. That is what makes the tragedy of human history, and always prevents human sin from becoming an insignificant and squalid thing. To reassert the fatherhood and childhood as an unlost truth, and to re-establish its power as the central fact of life ; to tell men that they were, and to make them actually be, the sons of God, — that was the purpose of the coming of Jesus, and the shaping power of His life.

Of course it is not possible to speak of such an idea — which is indeed the idea of the universe — as if it were a message intrusted to the Son of God when He came to be the Savior of mankind. It was not only something which He knew and taught ; it was something which He was. No other truth ever so inspires a merely human teacher, so fills his whole life with itself, so comes to be not merely the creed which his lips declare but the life which his whole living utters, as this truth of man's childhood to God. And in

Him who was at once the manifested God and the completion of humanity, the idea and the person are so mingled that we cannot separate them. He is the truth, and whoever receives Him becomes the son of God.

As I read the Gospels and see what Jesus is trying to do with men, it seems to me as if this truth that man is the child of God were to him, in a certain genuine sense, a final truth, — a truth beyond which the soul cannot or at least need not go, — a truth which, if it could be really laid upon the soul, would bring its own evidence and its own interpretation. It is indeed capable of being analyzed. It may be resolved into the several elements which make up its meaning. It includes the notions of a common nature between the Father and the son, of a spontaneous affection of the Father, of an essential obligation of the son, and of a possibility of the son's unlimited growth into the Father's likeness. All these are present, are assumed in every declaration of man's sonship to God which Jesus ever makes. But He does not unfold them and define them. It seems to Him as if, when He says to any human creature, "You are God's child," all these included truths revealed themselves to the soul in such degree as his spiritual nature was then able to receive them. It seems to Him as if when He says to a sinner, forgetful of his sonship, " Rise up and be God's child," all these included truths came in with their own power to restore his life. He always treats the truth of Fatherhood as the best children of the best earthly fathers treat it, not ignorant of the elemental truths of which it is composed, but best satisfied to let it rest in its own unity, as if any analysis must disturb its beauty and its power.

It is more important than we often think, that we should grasp the general idea, the general purpose, of the life of Jesus. The Gospels become to us a new book when we no longer read them merely as the anecdotes of the life of one who, with a great, kind heart, went through the world promiscuously doing good as opportunities occurred to Him. The drifting and haphazard currents gather themselves together, and we are borne on with the full and enthusiastic impulse of a great river which knows itself and knows the sea it seeks. And when the ruling idea is this which fills the life of Jesus, it is doubly true that only by clearly seizing it can we get at the heart and meaning of His life. For it is not only an idea; it is a religious inspiration. It is not only the food of the mind; it is the fire of the soul. In all its human uses, the idea of fatherhood comes nearer to being a religious idea than that of any other human relationship. And when we catch sight of it as the expression of man's relationship to God, it has all that mysterious and beautiful mingling of the most vast and awful with the most near and personal and urgent, all that vagueness which we know includes definiteness, all that definiteness not excluding vagueness, which is the very essence of religious impressiveness. And when we think of it as the idea of Jesus, it must always have this special beauty connected with it, that Jesus must have grown up into the apprehension of it as He grew into the consciousness of His own life. He must have become aware that all men were God's sons, and felt the desire to tell them so and make their sonship a reality, kindling like fire within Him, just in proportion as He came to know, softly and gradually, under the skies of Galilee and the roof of the carpenter, the deep and absorbing mystery that He himself was the Son of God.

It is not my purpose to prove here that this which I have given is a true statement of the idea of Jesus. As He stands there in the broad sunlight of the Gospels, as His clear words come down to us through the atmosphere of centuries which His spirit has purified, I do not see how any one can have a doubt of what He means by standing there, what the purpose of His life is as He himself conceives it. If any man had a doubt, I should only want to open the Gospels with him at four most solemn places. Here is the consummate teaching of Jesus. In His favorite form of parable, with the widest gaze across the vast field of man, with the most profound and sad and hopeful sympathy with human life, He tells His story of the Prodigal Son. It is the everlasting picture of the double possibilities of man, — obedience and disobedience. The old parable of Eden, the present mystery of your life and mine, the far-off Judgment Day, and the great White Throne, are all gathered in together and are lying in the crystal depths of that story. And lo! these two possibilities live in the house of one great Fatherhood. "A certain man had two sons," and from the embrace of that father's love neither of the two sons ever departs. Or, if this seems too metaphorical to be the revelation of Christ's idea of man, turn to another scene, and hear Him teaching all men to pray, "Our Father who art in heaven." Not only the needy child, who is going in a moment to beg for his daily bread, but the sinful child, whose lip is already trembling with the prayer to be forgiven, begins his petition with the claim of the son upon the father. In that idea alone the possibility and privilege of prayer grow clear. Or, still more solemn in its special circumstances, there is the scene beside the tomb from which He has just risen, when He draws back the curtain, and with one word proclaims His life and His disciples' life together. "I ascend unto my Father and to your Father," He declares. And when He has ascended, and years have passed away, and all that He did and was have grown familiar to the disciple who loved Him most and knew Him best; when that disciple sums up all his conception of the life of Jesus, what he says is only this : " To as many as received Him, to them gave He power to become the sons of God." Surely, we cannot be wrong if we say positively that to Christ himself the truth that man was God's child by nature was the great fact of man's existence; and the desire that man might be God's child in reality was the motive of His own life and work.

I have dwelt long upon this opening explanation. But I must leave it now. My design, in these lectures, is to try to show how this idea of Jesus, inspiring and presented through his personality, becomes the shaping power of men's lives I want to trace its presence in all of the higher regions of man's life. I want to see how it influences man's doing of duty, and his relation to his fellow-men, and his acceptance of pain or pleasure, and his treatment of his own intellectual powers These are my four lectures

Man in his various life, touched and influenced and shaped and led by the Fatherhood of God, revealed and renewed to him by Jesus. To-day I shall speak of man's moral life. The second lecture will be of the child of God in all his social existence. The next lecture will treat of his relation to enjoyment and suffering, which are the right hand and the left hand of the same Father. And in the last lecture I shall speak of that life of the intellect in which man is most ready to forget his Father, or to think that his Father has nothing that he can do for him. They will be Biblical studies; for I shall look solely to what Jesus, the revealer of the Father, did for men in the few years of which the Gospels tell, in order to find the types of what it is His perpetual effort and wish to do. I dare to hope, as the result of all our studies, that we may be helped somewhat in that which I think we all find the hardest and most hopeless work of all our lives, — the effort to keep our highest ideas and our commonest occupations in constant and healthy contact with each other.

Forgive me one word more. It gives me also

pleasure to believe that the subject which I have chosen is one which would not have been unwelcome to my dear friend of years ago, whose honored name this lectureship bears, and in whose behalf I shall in some sort speak. For, of the men whom I have known, there has been none whose daily moral life, whose association with his fellow-men, whose meeting of the joy and pain of living, and whose ways of thought and study, have been more in the power of the idea of Jesus, more inspired by his Lord's revelation that he was, more obedient and trustful to his Lord's authority in order that he might become, the son of God.

The manifestation of God's fatherhood which was made in Jesus is the shaping power of Christian morals, — that which makes the morality of Christian life distinct and different from any other that the world has seen. In what does that difference consist? In two things, as it seems to me: First, in the complete combination of pattern and power in the source from which the morality proceeds; and, second, in the combination of reason and authority in the basis upon which the morality is constantly recognized as resting. These are the two great characteristics of family morality, of that rectitude and goodness which grow up in the child as he lives in his father's house, sheltered by and fed out of his father's character. Think of them both for a moment. Where, except in that primal type of human influence and benefaction, the human family, do the pattern of goodness and the power of goodness meet in such perfect unity? Elsewhere there may stand up models of excellence, but they are distant and cold. They do not carry in themselves their own enforcement. They are not clothed with the impressiveness of a deep natural affection. Elsewhere than in the home there may be very winning persuasions to goodness; but nowhere so perfectly as in the home does the persuasive appeal come from the mouth of the very goodness which is the natural pattern of the life which it tries to win. The good father at once shows goodness as no other being can show it to the child, and likewise invites him to it with an influence that no other being can possess. And, besides this, the child, when he has come to goodness like his father's by obedience to his father, finds himself unable to tell whether the good life which he tries to live is something which holds him by its own inherent fascination, or something to which he submits in willing acceptance of his father's will. The essential and the arbitrary blend, and are lost in one another. The child's nature bears witness to its oneness with the father's nature by the way in which it makes its own choices those duties which come to it in the first place as the father's mandates.

Now these two qualities, shadowed forth in every true home, come to their completeness in the home of God, the home of man in God, which is Christianity. It will be interesting, I hope, to follow this truth out in some detail; but first we can see, perhaps, how true it is, if we turn suddenly to our Gospels and open them at once at what is, after all, the great text-book of Christian morals, the code of Christian life, the correspondent and fulfilment in the New Testament of the Ten Commandments in the Old. I mean the Sermon on the Mount. To that discourse let us give a few moments' study. In the late summer, Jesus is coming home from one of his teaching-tours in Galilee, and in the evening he and the company that follow him approach Capernaum. They will not enter the city till tomorrow morning. To-night the people sleep around the foot of a great hill that rises near the town. But Jesus, that he may be more alone, climbs higher, and spends the night in prayer and meditation. Out of this solitude, out of this mysterious communion with His Father, in which He has, as it were, refilled Himself with the assurance that the human is son to the Divine, He comes when morning breaks, and, gathering His disciples around Him, He speaks to them, and the multitude who have thronged about Him, the Sermon on the Mount, which is written in three chapters of St. Matthew's Gospel. I do not see how any one who reads it carefully can fail to feel that in that sermon we have what is essentially a unit, — one single, separate discourse of Jesus. It has no rhetorical order or progress. It does not move in any argumentative development. We have but to feel ourselves back into the bright air and sunshine of that fresh morning far away in Galilee, with the sweet distraction of the early birds filling the air, and the soft, dreamy faces of the Galilean peasants making the listening group, in order to become aware how perfectly impossible it was that the discourse should move to any such measure as might have become the lecture-room of a new Rabbi. It has its unity in its controlling purpose. It is one by the life-blood of the one idea which beats through it, and which those ready and responsive peasant natures feel. And what is that idea? Neander calls the Sermon on the Mount "the Magna Charta of the kingdom of God." It is a fine phrase, and in one sense it is completely true. But really the idea of God which fills the great discourse is not the idea of king, but the idea of father. No doubt the two, in their original use and in the loftiest use of them, when, as in the loftiest use of all words, they refresh the lost memory of their origin, are really one. The king was originally father. The Basileia was a family. It belonged to the king,

On the Moral Life of Man. 27

as the family belongs to the father, by right of blood. It was not like the Turannis, which implied a usurpation, an unnatural and cruel thing. Kingship included the three essential ideas of fatherhood, which, as I reminded you, are oneness of nature, natural impulse of obedience, and the obligation of loving care. The noblest heathen always felt all this; and Zeus is either king of gods and men, or father of gods and men,—as if the two names meant the selfsame thing. But yet the two words always tended to drift apart. Lordship and command belonged to kingship; love and care belonged to fatherhood. What we really have, then, in the Sermon on the Mount, what gives it its great, everlasting value, is the passing over of kingship into fatherhood; or, if you please to put it so, the opening and deepening of kingship till it reveals the fatherhood which lies folded at the heart of it. This, I am sure, is the key of the Sermon on the Mount which alone can unlock its meaning. Men have often pointed out how largely its separate precepts can be matched out of other codes; as if the substance and power of a moral law lay in its commandments, and did not really rest in the conception of the commander which breathed through it and gave it life.

Here, then, is what the Sermon on the Mount really means. And, in conformity with this, all through it there are strung those two great combinations which I spoke of, — the combination of pattern and power, the combination of reason and authority. The pattern is a personal nature, ultimate and absolute, behind which it is impossible to go. The good is good because it is like Him. The bad is bad because it is unlike Him. There is no other standard in the whole discourse than that. It is assumed that a man may know God and then that he wants nothing more, that in God he has the perfect test and touchstone of all life. "Be ye therefore perfect," Jesus says, "even as your Father which is in heaven is perfect." "Love your enemies, bless them that curse you"; and why? "That ye may be the children of your Father which is in heaven." "Seek ye first the kingdom of God and His righteousness, and all these things shall be added unto you." What do these words mean, that close like a great choral amen the sweet and rhythmical injunctions to a divine carelessness? "Take no thought for your life." "Lay not up treasures on the earth." "Take no thought, saying, What shall we eat, or what shall we drink." Let all things go. Only,— and then the words seem to concentrate out of their easy carelessness into a deep intensity that is all the more intense by contrast,— only, "seek God's righteousness, seek to be righteous like Him, with that divine capacity of likeness which is in you, as His children, and then everything else shall follow as it may." These are no solitary texts. They are only special words in which the whole current of the sermon flashes up into peculiar distinctness, as a wave flashes on the bosom of a stream and shows which way the stream is running.

And as the Father is the standard of the moral life that is enforced, so it is from Him and from His fatherhood that the whole power comes by which that standard is to be pursued and finally attained. There is nothing abstract and cold. Everything shines and burns with personal affection. I am to be good like my Father; I am to be good because of my Father; like His character, because of His love. "If ye forgive men their trespasses, then your Heavenly Father will forgive you." "Swear not by heaven, for it is God's throne, nor by earth, for it is His footstool." "Let your light shine before men, that they may glorify your Father which is in heaven." "Blessed are the peace-makers, for they shall be called the children of God." These, again, are not exceptional or accidental words. They are the flashes on the stream which flows the other way to meet the stream from God to man which we were just now tracing. Already it is true, as by and by an Apostle will declare, that "of Him, and through Him, and to Him, are all things." The pattern descends from the Father to the Son. The responsive likeness goes back from the Son to the Father; and both because they are Father and Son to one another. It is all full of the spirit of spontaneousness. It is "the Magna Charta of the kingdom of God," indeed. But the picture fails if we think of the reluctant king upon the plain at Runnymede with his stern barons compelling him to give what he gave only with hatred and rage. Rather it seems to be the prophecy and anticipation of that heavenly plain where the celestial King in the mystic picture of the Revelation gives Himself ungrudgingly to His beloved, whose natures, perfectly redeemed by Him and conformed to His, can take Him perfectly; where "the Lamb which is in the midst of the throne shall feed them, and shall lead them unto living fountains of waters,"—the anticipation of that and the memory and completion of the garden at the other end of human history, where the Father walked with his children in their first innocence.

Along with this combination the Sermon on the Mount always keeps the other,—the combination of reason and authority, or of essentialness and arbitrariness, which is characteristic of the child's obedience to the father. I must not dwell on this, but I am sure that all of us have felt, as we have read those sacred chapters of St. Matthew, how exquisitely these two lights play through them and harmonize with one another,—the light that comes to any duty from the command of God that we should do it, and the light which the same duty wins because we ourselves perceive that it is the right thing to do. The essence of every beatitude is in the human heart, and yet the human heart loves to hear the utterance of the beatitudes from the mouth of God as if they were His arbitrary enactments. I know by that of the nature of God which is in me as His child, that they which hunger and thirst after righteousness shall certainly be filled. I am sure by that subtle knowledge of Him which the child must have of the Father, that He could not leave a really longing soul unsatisfied in all His world. That importunate happiness, eager to give itself away, must pour itself into every ready life. But yet I accept the utterance which Jesus makes of that which I already knew, as a genuine revelation. The instinct of my wakened childhood rests upon the strong confirmation of the Father's uttered word. This runs through all the great discourse. I leave it with you to trace it there. Only I want you to notice that this interplay of essentialness and arbitrariness is exactly what characterizes every true home life, where the children learn truth and receive commandments from their father. The child's partial and growing perception that it must be so, chimes and harmonizes with the father's distinct injunction that it shall be so.

I am sure that when the listening repose of the multitude was broken as the sermon closed, and, like a melted stream, the crowd flowed away into the city, the people carried something more with them than a few handfuls of good precepts. I think that they went silently, or with few words, with something of exaltation and wonder at themselves in their faces. They had been taught that they were God's children. One who was evidently God's Son Himself had told them so. He had bidden them, as God's children, at once to see duty with something of His own immediateness of perception, and also to hear Him announcing it to them out of a Father's lips. Duty, the thing they ought to do, had shone for them that morning at once with its own essential sweetness and with the illumination of their Father's will. No wonder that as they walked together they said to one another, "He speaks to us with authority. It is not like the Scribes."

I must not linger on this hurried study of the Sermon on the Mount. I have dwelt thus long upon it because, as it is the longest and most deliberate statement of moral duty in the Gospels, I wanted to show how it was all pervaded by and built about the idea of Jesus. Let us go on now to see how that idea pervades likewise all His treatment of the men and women whom His life touched. It is the idea of a divine fatherhood, of a natural belonging of every man's soul in goodness, of wickedness as an exile, an unnatural, unfilial state of life, and of the return to goodness as the coming back to a homeland which the soul recognizes as it enters into it and claims as its true place. I think that this idea of morals at once outgoes and comprehends the various theories of moral life which men have framed and set in opposition to each other. If in the family the child's instinct of childhood unites in itself the perception of his own best good with the consciousness of obligation to his Father's will, then in the world, turned by Christ's revelation to one mighty family, the utilitarian and the intuitional theories of duty may blend in harmony, and the soul serving God as its Father may live under the combined power of the two.

But, not to dwell on this, the idea of Jesus applied to men's moral life must include two things, — a revelation of the moral standard, and a revelation of the moral motive. Let us take these in their order.

And first, the moral standard. What is it? What am I to be conformed to as the work of moral improvement goes on in me? There may be various answers. One man may say, "To this law," holding up a scroll of precepts. "That is to be your goal. When you obey those, the work is done." Another man says, "To this person," pointing to some one, human or divine, whose life is moving along outside of mine, — a pattern, a model, which I am to emulate as a candle measures its twinkling light against a star. Now the answer of Jesus is different from both of these, I think. "You are to be like your Father," He declares; "but it is in the fact that He is your Father and that you are His child that the possibility of likeness lies, and that the kind of possible likeness is decreed. You are to be like Him, as the child is like the father, by the attainment of that echo of the father's nature which is the child's essential heritage. You are to be like Him by coming to that expression of Him which is the true idea of your child-life. You are to fulfil the unfulfilled programme of your own life, which is involved in the fact that you are the child of God. You are to become 'like your Father,' fulfilling the injunction of the Sermon on the Mount by 'coming to yourself,' so realizing the picture of the parable of the Prodigal Son."

Is there here an intelligible and practicable moral standard? Man is to return into the idea of his own life as the son of God. He is to be equal to his own conception, as that conception is written in the nature of the Holy Being from whom he came and to whom he belongs. At least, that is a standard whose perpetual presence shaped our Lord's treatment of the men and women whom He was trying to restore. Note this in several particulars. First, look at the combination of sternness and kindliness, of mercy and severity, which appears wherever Jesus touches a sinner's life. One day they brought to Him a woman taken in the act of sin. Their stern, hard faces — the faces of the Scribes and Pharisees — glared at their victim, and then turned away from her to Him from whom they claimed her condemnation. "Moses in the Law commanded us that such should be stoned," they said. It was purely the reference to a law, to the appraisal of a sin by its assigned, appointed penalty. There is no thought of her, no consideration of what she is, or of what she possibly may be. It is only the sin, the law, and Moses, the appraiser of sins and laws by the standards of an absolute justice that is as impersonal and as free from obtrusive sympathies as the stars or winds. Then Jesus turns and looks around upon them all. He lets a silence fall through the great temple while He stoops and seems to write upon the ground. It is as if He wanted a gap, a blank of stillness, to come between their view about it all and His. Then He speaks: "He that is without sin among you, let him first cast a stone at her." Do you not see the difference? Everything is personal. It is not "such as she," it is she. They are not mere mechanical executors of a written law; they are men who cannot escape personal judgments themselves. They have something to do with her besides to stone her. They are partners in sin. They are beings with the same obligations, the same temptations, the same history of failure. The whole pulsates with personality. And when, after the Scribes and Pharisees have crept away, He turns to the woman and says, "I do not condemn thee: go, and sin no more,"—along with a deep and terrible sense of how dreadfully she had sinned, along with the most complete self-condemnation, there must have come into the poor creature's heart a vision of the power of not sinning which was in her, in which she thenceforth could believe because He believed in it, and in the conscious possession of which she knew herself to be, in the first unlost but long unseen idea and deepest truth of her existence, the child of God. Or think about the other woman, who came creeping in, with her box of ointment, to anoint the feet of Jesus as He sat supping with the

Pharisee. The same contrast of treatment shines out there. The shocked and scandalized Pharisee cries out, " This man ought to have known who and what manner of woman this is ! " It is " what manner of woman." She is one of a class. She is a kind of being, not a being, not one live, loving, despairing woman. But Jesus begins to speak, and instantly there she is ! No longer this " manner of woman," but " this woman." And then her story comes, — the story of her love for her rescuer, and of her humble and absorbing and self-forgetful desire to do something for Him ; the story of her tears and kisses on His feet, and the spilt ointment whose fragrance yet filled the room. And it is told so that the most supercilious guests turn with a wondering recognition of a true human life among them ; told so that the poor woman herself, while she cowered with shame and glowed with love, must have thrilled through and through with self-recognition, with a knowledge of herself wholly new but perfectly certain and clear ; told so that no figure of woman's nature anywhere in history stands more clearly before the eyes of men to-day. And it is her possibility, undestroyed by all her sin; it is her power of loving the manifestation of God, — the power by which she may rise out of her sin and be what she was made to be, — it is this that He touches by His words and calls forth into life, and by its new life saves her soul, which seemed to be lost and dead.

In both these stories see the severity and see the gentleness! There is no making light of sin; there is no cruelty to the sinner. These two hands, one strong with stern holiness, the other gentle with sympathy, untwist the cords that bind the soul, and set it free to be itself. The rebuked sin becomes itself the impulse that sends the soul away from its sin into the revealed possibility of goodness. And these two hands they are which always Christ has used to rescue men's souls. The perfect severity of holiness and the perfect tenderness of love, which blend nowhere but in the thought of the ideal family, blend perfectly in the moral method of the Son of God seeking His brethren.

Again, I think that this same idea appears in the way in which Jesus uses *self-sacrifice*, — that instrument which all the moral disciplines that the world has seen have always used, but of which He always seems to make a higher and peculiar use. One kind of moral training uses self-sacrifice as punishment. Because you have done so much which you ought not to have done, therefore you shall surrender so much which it would give you pleasure to possess. Another uses self-sacrifice as an expression of the essential badness of the thing surrendered. Because the earth is inherently, intrinsically wicked, therefore come away from it and be separate. Because the body is accursed, therefore pluck out thy right eye, cut off thy right hand. But to Jesus self-sacrifice always is a means of freedom. That is what always gives to the self-denials which He demands a triumphant and enthusiastic air. Not because you have not deserved to enjoy it, not because it is wicked to enjoy it, but because there is another enjoyment more worthy of your nature, for which the native appetite shall show itself in you the moment that you really lay hold of it, therefore let this first inferior enjoyment go; and by this conception of the purpose of self-sacrifice, Christ's law and limit of self-sacrifice is always settled. One day a young man came to Jesus. He had seen some glimpse of Jesus's idea. He dreamed that he might be a son of God. "What shall I do that I may reach eternal life?" he said. And Jesus lifted His finger and pointed out to him the long line of milestones that marked the way to his celestial aspiration,—humanity, purity, honesty, brotherly love. They did not satisfy the youth. He knew them all, and yet he did not get at what he wanted, what he dreamed of. "All these have I done. What lack I yet?" His soul was like a boat tied fast, but tied with a long rope. It was able to struggle up the channel, past headland and light and buoy that marked the way; but always something held it back from perfectly laying itself at rest beside the golden shore. "What lack I yet? What lack I yet?" And then said Jesus, "Go and sell all that thou hast, and thou shalt have treasure in heaven; and come and follow me." He did not say, "You do not deserve wealth." He did not say, "It is wicked to be rich." He only said,

"You will be free if you are poor, and then I can lead you to the Father, in whom you shall find yourself." He went back, past the buoys and headlands, down the bay to where the rope was tied, and cut the boat loose from its anchorage. The sadness with which the young man went away one would fain believe was the sadness of the rescued slave, who misses and mourns for the familiar fetter, even while his heart begins already to open to the embrace of the new life of liberty that spreads bewilderingly, almost awfully before him.

I mention only one more indication of the fact that the standard which the morality of Jesus sets up is something far more intimate than a law of abstract right and wrong, or the example of a person between whom and us there is no essential and indestructible relationship. It is found in the vehement and passionate reaction which his teachings and rebukes excited. Jesus went about the cities which lined the upper shores of the Sea of Galilee. He told the people of their sins. He offered them the new life of obedience to Him. Instantly there was an outbreak. They did not just ignore Him. He did not merely seem to them an enthusiast, whom they could brush aside out of the reality that filled their practical life. They were betrayed into that last rage which no man feels until he is fighting with the highest idea of himself, the last and most desperate battle of the human soul. Jesus sees this, and there is pity burning through and under His indignation as He cries, " Thou Capernaum, which art exalted unto heaven, shalt be cast down to hell." It is the heaven where Capernaum belongs that makes the tragedy of the hell which she chooses. And so, when the Gadarenes begged the intrusive miracle-worker to depart out of their coasts ; or when the congregation of the synagogue at Nazareth sprang up in rage when Jesus preached to them ; or when the cry of blasphemy arose at the sight of the divine power that was in Him passing beyond the work of healing lameness, and beginning to claim its holier and dearer privilege of forgiving sins ; or when, unseen, unheard, in many a brooding heart and many a suspicious whisper that vented its querulous maliciousness in the country lanes and cottages, or in the palaces or hovels of Jerusalem, the tide of hatred slowly gathered which broke out at last with "Crucify him! crucify him!" before Pilate's judgment seat, and raged in taunts and jeers around the cross, — through all these scenes there is no sufficient explanation of it all, until you get down to that seat wherein the deepest power of mortification and of rage resides, a wounded and wronged conscience. It was the national consciousness which, under that strange mingling of nationality and individuality which was the very genius of Judaism, meant likewise the consciousness of every man, the consciousness that the people was the people of God, that every man in it was the son of God, — it was this consciousness, summoned to life by the presence among them of the Son of God, that rose and beat against the low conditions of the life under which they had buried it, and made the tempest whose hoarse tumult we hear everywhere behind the gentle voice of Jesus as we open the Gospel doors.

This, then, I take to be the beginning of the Gospel of the Son of God. It is the renewal of the divine consciousness in every man as the standard by which he is to be judged. And the power of that renewal is the Incarnation. "The Word was made flesh and dwelt among us"; and, "to as many as received Him, to them gave He power to become the sons of God." This is surely the moral power of that which Jesus, when He talks with Nicodemus, calls the "being born again." The Pharisee wonders. It seems to him as if the new-found Rabbi told him something unnatural, something against the course of nature. It seems to be a going back. "Can a man enter a second time into his mother's womb and be born?" And Jesus answers: "Yes, it is a going back, only back much farther than you think, — much farther than the mother's womb. It must be a birth from heaven, taking you back into heaven again. It must be a birth from God, restoring in you the first idea of your existence, that you are His child. You can enter into the kingdom of heaven only as, beneath all its obscurations and accumulated hindrances, that idea is stirred to life, and you are born at once out of the highest heights of God and into the deepest depths of yourself."

Surely such an idea of man makes abundantly simple that which has often seemed so hard to understand. I mean the way in which righteousness and men's struggles to be good have always refused to be confined to the limits of any specific culture or even to those who knew the name of Christ. Everywhere throughout the world, everywhere throughout the ages, men have sought holiness. The best and noblest men everywhere have always been true seekers after God. That is inexplicable if Christianity is a new power, a new gift to the faculties of man, nay, as it often seems to be stated, a new set of faculties in man which he has not possessed before. But how entirely explicable, how natural it is, if what the Incarnation did was to redeem men into what was their original and undestroyed nature and privilege! What wonder that the hidden sonship should have been forever flashing forth wherever the crust of earthliness and sensuality and selfishness was thinnest! How divinely, as the dream and hope of all the best souls that had ever lived, as "the desire of all nations," comes at last the Son of God "to take away sin by the sacrifice of Himself," by wondrous and unutterable pain so to make manifest the love of God that man's selfishness might be broken into fragments, and the divine idea of humanity which had flashed forth through cracks should glow in one unhindered glory over all the redeemed life of man.

There is not one word of the argument for righteousness on abstract principles, or on the ground of its utility, in all the Gospels. Jesus and Socrates are absolutely incomparable. They start from different points. They journey by different roads. They come in sight of one another when their separate journeys mount to their highest elevations. They travel in the same direction, but they do not travel together. The one reveals; the other argues. And it is certainly true of Jesus that the Christian's eagerness to show that all good and all methods for all good were embodied in Him has obscured the definite and single method which He did use to bring men into the service of duty. "I am the Son of God" He said. "Yet I am one with you. You, too, are the sons of God. His image, all blurred and stained, is in you. Let me set it free, restore it, redeem it; and then you shall live by the law of your own renewed wills. The pattern shall be in your hearts when those hearts once more are pure. The image of God, manifest first in Me, and from Me reawakened in your own filial consciousness, — that is the pattern of your life, the standard of your duty."

And so we are ready now for the second point of which I wished to speak. Nothing is so imperfect, nothing, indeed, is so melancholy, so tragical, as a pattern set before a man which he has no power to attain. It is like a boat at sea with the best compass in the world on board, but neither oars nor sails. The faithful needle tells its story; there is no doubt which way we ought to sail; but there we lie, tossing up and down, without progress, or drifted only by the stupid sea on which we float. Along with the revelation of the Divine pattern in Christ finding its echo in the people's selves to whom He spoke, there must have come some motive, some stimulus to follow and attain the pattern which He set; and that, the more we read the Gospels, it grows evident to us was just as simple and just as peculiarly His own as was the setting up of the pattern. The motive, too, was wholly personal, and was all based upon man's filialness. It was purely and solely the elevation to its highest power of that same force which, in the human family, causes the father's life to be repeated in the child's. We call it love; but we must remember that full love always has two elements, and we must be sure that we keep both of them in our thought when we speak of the power by which the human life is shaped into the image of the Divine. Love is at once admiration and affection. We often separate the two. We talk of loving some poor creature in whom there is nothing admirable. We talk of loving some cold statue which makes no appeal to our affection. But really these are only mangled parts of love. True love, complete love, finely combines a pure, unselfish perception of the essential quality of a character with a warm personal gratitude for what that character bestows on us. The perception of absolute quality saves it from foolish fondness, and the gratitude rescues it from being the mere dilettanteism of the connoisseur. It is a love like this which makes the power of Christian morals. Look, for instance, at that great event in which the whole life and work of the Savior found its completion. I mean His crucifixion. I do not speak now of the essential mystery which is in that wonderful event. I count alike foolish and short-sighted the two men, both of whom try to eliminate and scatter the mysteriousness of the cross of Christ, one of them by saying that there is no peculiar and special character in that strange and single death, the other by dissecting its power into its elements and trying to account for all its force. I know that the death of the beggar, the death of the baby, has in it a mystery of force which no wisest man can comprehend. I know that He whose life was one with the baby's and the beggar's, and yet infinitely deeper, vaster, must have had a mystery in His death over which eternity shall keep guard, husbanding its treasures, and giving them forth to the eternally ripening soul as it shall need and shall be able to receive them. He who tells me that he will read to me now the mystery of the death of Jesus, shuts my ears with his very offer. I will not let him tear for me the mystery of the dawn which no hand can hasten as it slowly brightens to the full morning. And so it is not of the essential mystery of Christ's powerful death, but of its immediate moral power that I speak. It is the great renewing spectacle of human life. When men look at it, there comes up out of their hearts the pattern of divinity which is there, their sonship to the Holy One; and to attain that holiness, to realize it perfectly, becomes the passion of their lives. And it is love for the Sufferer which makes that passion, — love with its two perfect elements perfectly combined. It is admiration for what He is doing, the unselfishness, the heroism, the godlike patience. And it is gratitude because He is doing it for us. It is these two that blend into the passionate devotion with which a man, in the great phrase of the Gospels, "follows after Christ," — seeks, that is, with his own essential sonship, to realize in himself the sonship of the Son of God.

One loves to think, nay, one rejoices to be sure,

that under all the most artificial — shall we not say under all the most fantastic? — theories which men have framed and held concerning the power of the death of Jesus, this sweet and reasonable influence proceeding from it has always done its blessed work. With silent, soft, and mighty pressure, the sight of the Sufferer's holiness and the gratitude for the Sufferer's pity, as one complete power, one perfect love, has drawn the depths of men's lives on to the nature of the Sufferer, and there their oneness to Him has become known to them, and they, in and through Him, have been renewed into the image of their Father and His Father. The robber who was crucified with Him felt that power first. It was a baptism of blood, and the power which our baptisms re-echo found its first utterance in him. "Being by nature born in sin and the child of wrath," there by the fellowship of suffering, there by the power of love, in which admiration and gratitude met, he was made the "child of grace."

Let us trace now, if I have defined it clearly, some of the qualities which this inherent character of the Christian impulse imprints upon the Christian morality. And first of all I name that union of discontent and hope which, in the first disciples, and in all who have followed in their footsteps, has always marked the progress of the Christian's moral life. Remember one more scene in the rich Gospels. It is once more the Sea of Galilee. Simon Peter, — that transparent nature in whom we are able to trace, as in the simplest organism, those changes and reactions which become obscure and hard to trace in structures that are more complete and complicated, — Simon Peter has Jesus in his little fishing-boat. And this time it is by some exhibition of His power, by some wonderful draught of fishes in the before empty net, that the personality of the Master has been pressed close upon His disciple. And then Peter breaks out. Prostrate at Jesus's knees, "Depart from me," he cries, "for I am a sinful man, O Lord!" Despondency, almost despair, a deep sight into his own heart, a bitter sense of contrast with the nature which the touch of miracle, like a flash of lightning, had made clear to him, — all this is in those passionate and hurried words. But what comes next? "When they had brought their ships to land, they forsook all and followed Him." Peter and all the rest! Not only all the rest, but Peter! With the imploring cry, "Depart!" yet on his lips, he follows Him whom he had begged to go away. It was the power of love overwhelming the sense of unworthiness, and filling him with hope. It was the noble, beautiful inconsequence and inconsistence of a great nature all in tumult, which never felt the attraction of holiness so irresistibly as when it seemed altogether beyond his reach, and never so knew how unholy he was as at the very moment when the power of holiness was making him its slave and chaining him, a willing follower and servant, to the feet of the Holy One. Nothing but personal love can hold and harmonize that inconsistency. Only in the complete devotion of a soul that sees in the apparently unattainable that which it knows, by a sense beyond all reason, by a movement of its own profoundest consciousness, that it can and must attain, — nothing but that could have made strength out of such weakness, and hope out of the very substance of despair.

Again, I think that Christ's whole use of punishments and threats is characteristic of the idea on which His whole moral treatment of humanity proceeds. A tyrant uses threats and punishments for restriction, desiring to repress that which is mischievous and bad. A parent, if he is truly parental, and not at all tyrannical, uses threats and punishments as means of revelation and enfranchisement, that he may set free for their own higher action a knowledge and ability which is held in prison. The blows of one are struck to bind the fetters tight; the other's blows are struck to loose the fetters, that the limbs' native powers may go free. What are the blows of Jesus? He sends out His disciples to do His work, to preach His gospel; and He declares to them what shall be the penalty of unfaithfulness and partial, compromising consecration. "He that loveth father or mother more than me is not worthy of me. He that loveth son or daughter more than me is not worthy of me. He that findeth his life shall lose it." But instantly, — part of the same verse, — before He takes His breath, He cries, "He that loseth his life for My sake shall find it." The threat is nothing to Him. He does not care to inspire fear unless, startled and stirred by danger, the men to whom He speaks can be made to tremble down so deep that the capacity of being all that He wants them to be shall wake out of its slumber and stand upon its feet, and, shaking the very thought of fear away, go forth to a duty which has its only inspiration in the consciousness of privilege and in the thought of blessing. He always shakes the sleepy soul, not as the jailer, who rouses the wretch upon his execution morning, to lead him to his death, but as the watchman, who puts the sword into the drowsy soldier's hand that he may go and fight his battle. It is as a revelation of blessing by the dreadfulness of its opposite. It is as the golden medal shown on its reverse, with all its deep depressions only indicating the promontories of happiness and goodness which its true face contains. It is thus that Jesus always threatens men with punishment. The tutor of a French prince, I have read, used to tie a rod to the child's sash when he had deserved to be punished for a fault. It was an appeal to his princeliness. It was the suggestion and reminder of how a prince ought to behave. It was an appeal to his native nobility, and not to his fear of pain. It seems to me as if every threatening of Christ were an appeal to the native princeliness of man, to his royal nature as the son of the King of kings, a sacred being to whom sin is eternally unnatural and punishment a dreadful anomaly and shame.

And yet again I find the same meaning in the wise and measured use which Jesus always makes of the machinery of duty and of the forms of righteousness in their relation to the impulse of duty and the purpose of righteousness. These last are never for a moment lost from sight. The kingliness of the impulse, the subordination of the instrument and the form, are never allowed to become obscure. An abandonment of all forms and outward instruments is very easy. A true adjustment of them to the unseen purposes which they subserve is as rare as it is hard, as hard as it is rare. It is in the healthiest and truest family life that their balance is most perfectly preserved. And when the Lord insists on celebrating His profound spiritual consecration by being baptized in Jordan; when, in His kingliness, He does not refuse to pay His tribute; when He sends the poor leper, who is already cured, to get his warrant of restored health from the priest; when He bids His disciples observe and do whatsoever the Pharisees who sit in Moses's seat shall bid them do, — in all these cases it is the law of the family life which He is laying down to them, the law which reaches back to the fact, but yet does not neglect the method, and through the form tries to shape the substance for its maturer life. It is the perfection of that instinct with which the dying Socrates, having left his rich legacy of spiritual teaching to his scholars, with his last breath bids them not forget the cock for Æsculapius, which was the formal type and expression of his piety.

I have only one more suggestion to offer on this head. There are words of Jesus, here and there, in which He distinctly sets His own faithfulness as the type and inspiration of the faithfulness which He expects of His disciples. Listen to the solemnity which is in His voice as, at the table of the Last Supper, He looks up into His Father's face and prays for these, His brethren. "As Thou has sent Me into the world, even so have I also sent them into the world. Sanctify them through Thy truth." Or, just before, looking directly into the disciples' eyes, "This is my commandment, that ye love one another as I have loved you." And yet again, "I in them and Thou in Me, that they all may be one in Us." Who can read words like these and not catch sight of what it was that was to fill these disciples' lives with energy, and to be the atmosphere wherein their new goodness should get all its growth? God's fatherhood to them made visible in Christ, His Son; their sonship to God made visible in Christ, their brother. It was as if, at the beginning of all the ages down which their Christian life has run, they lay, like Jacob on the night when he went out to his new life from his father's house, and to them, as to him. a ladder seemed to stretch up into heaven, and the angels of God ascended and descended on it, — the angels of duty bringing God's strength to men, and carrying men's obedience to God, on the ladder of the fatherhood and sonship that bound the heavens to the earth, set up in the new Beth-el, the new House of God, which was the life of Jesus.

It only remains that we should point out what must be some of the perpetual marks of a morality which is the outgrowth of such a faith as ours. Those marks belong to the Christian morality of all times. They are not separable from it. When we look into the future and see the goodness of humanity developing within the idea of Jesus, we must expect to see a greater and greater prominence of those marks in it. When we seek our own moral development from Him, we must look for it in the only kind which His method can bestow.

The first mark will be the prominence of what we may call the duties of sentiment. " Thou shalt love the Lord." " Thou shalt love thy brother." Thou shalt love. The duty of loving, — there is nothing of that in the codes of abstract duty. It is impossible to exclude that from its fundamental place in the system of duty whose constant spring is in the fatherhood of

God. But evidently this quality, this exaltation of the duty of sentiment over the duty of action, which makes the action valuable simply as an utterance of the sentiment, — this is a most important quality. It cannot be ignored. It gives the color and tone to all the morality which it pervades. It exposes that morality, no doubt, at the outset, to the charge and the danger of weakness and sentimentality, but in the end it gives it a buoyancy and elasticity and perpetual vitality which prophesy for it a permanence as endless as the Being in whose love it lives is everlasting; and so it is the one morality for which we can predict no end. Of this quality in duty it is no Christian's place to be ashamed or afraid. None of us may melt it away or sink it out of sight. In its prominence lies the soul of the duty that we do. We may not try to make that duty cold and soulless which has its true being in the central commandment which is its living soul, — "Thou shalt love."

Another mark of the Christian morality, the morality whose root is in the sonship of the soul to God, is the harmony with which it holds the absoluteness of goodness and the various responsibilities of men. It is full of discriminations which yet never tamper with the unchangeable sanctity of righteousness. As in the parable of Him from whom it all proceeds, so, in the life which that parable describes, the different talents of different servants are fully taken into the account. Duty is measured by chance, and yet the essential idea of duty is never weakened. I am bound to do less than you, but I am just as severely bound to do my little as you are to do your much. Where else could those ideas be kept in perfect harmony and peace, neither of them hurting the other, but within the larger idea of fatherhood? In what group could the child take his little task, fitted to his little hands, and do it, with the entire conviction that he must do it, and, nevertheless, not vexed nor bewildered by the sight of tasks a thousand times greater than his own being done close by his side; and, at the same time, the great man, the hero, dedicate himself to his vast work with no sense of oppression or injustice, nor with any feeling of superiority or pride, — in what group could these two faithful souls work on, in such difference and yet in such identity, but in a family where every child has his own special duty, great or small, clothed with the absoluteness of the Fatherhood which is over all? Where, but in the family idea of man, can these two necessary conceptions of the difference of duties and the absoluteness of duty meet in perfect peace?

I note again, as a characteristic of the morality of sonship, the way in which it secures humility by aspiration and not by depression. How to secure humility is the hard problem of all systems of duty. He who does work, just in proportion to the faithfulness with which he does it, is always in danger of self-conceit. Very often men seem to have given up the problem in despair, and they lavish unstinted praise upon the vigorous, effective worker without any qualifying blame of the arrogance with which he flaunts the duty that he does in the world's face. "The only way to make him humble," they would seem to say, "would be to make him idle. Let him stop doing duty and then, indeed, he might stop boasting. His arrogance is only the necessary price that the world and he pay for his faithfulness." To such a problem the Christian morality brings its vast conception of the universe. Above each man it sets the infinite life. The identity of nature between that life and his, while it enables him to emulate that life, compels him, also, to compare himself with it. The more zealously he aspires to imitate it, the more clearly he must encounter the comparison. The higher he climbs the mountain, the more he learns how the high mountain is past his climbing. It is the oneness of the soul's life with God's life that at once makes us try to be like Him and brings forth our unlikeness to Him It is the source at once of aspiration and humility. The more aspiration, the more humility. Humility comes by aspiration. If, in all Christian history, it has been the souls which most looked up that were the humblest souls; if to-day the rescue of a soul from foolish pride must be not by a depreciation of present attainment, but by opening more and more the vastness of the future possibility; if the Christian man keeps his soul full of the sense of littleness, even in all his hardest work for Christ, not by denying his own stature, but by standing up at his whole height, and then looking up in love and awe and seeing God tower into infinitude above him, — certainly all this stamps the morality which is wrought out within the idea of Jesus with this singular excellence, that it has solved the problem of faithfulness and pride, and made possible humility by aspiration.

And yet, once more, the morality of Jesus involves the only true secret of courage and of the freedom that comes of courage. More and more we come to see that courage is a positive thing. It is not simply the absence of fear. To be brave is not merely not to be afraid. Courage is that compactness and clear coherence of all a man's faculties and powers which makes his manhood a single operative unit in the world. That is the reason why narrowness of thought and life often brings a kind of courage, and why, as men's range of thought enlarges and their relations with their fellowmen increase, there often comes a strange timidity. The bigot is often very brave. He is held fast unto a unit, and possesses himself completely in his own selfishness. For such a bravery as that the man and the world both pay very dear. But when the grasp that holds a man and his powers is not his self-consciousness but his obedience to his Father, when loyalty to Him surrounds and aggregates the man's capacities, so that, held in His hand, the man feels his distinctiveness, his distinctive duty, his distinctive privilege, then you have reached the truth of which the bigot's courage was the imitation. Then you have secured courage, not by the limitation, but by the enlargement of the life. Then the dependence upon God makes the independence of man in which are liberty and courage. The man's own personality is found only in the household of his Father, and only in the finding of his personality does he come to absolute freedom and perfect fearlessness.

May I take a moment now before I close to recapitulate the points along the journey which we have travelled together to-night? We found the family character of Christian duty — the way in which it gathered its source out of the essential sonship of man to God — indicated in the meeting, first, of the pattern of righteousness and the power of righteousness; and, second, of reasonableness and authority in all the duty which the New Testament enjoins. This I tried to show you in the text-book of duty, the Sermon on the Mount.

Then I tried to show where the moral standard was put by Jesus. It is in the heart of every son of God made conscious of his sonship by the Son of God, who is Jesus.

Then we traced the nature of this standard as it was actually shown, first, in the combination of severity and goodness in the treatment of man by Jesus; second, in the character of His teaching about self-sacrifice; and third, in the vehement opposition and hatred which His life excited.

At the same time we saw that while this standard came to its full manifestation in Christianity, it had been struggling for utterance through all the religious life of man.

Passing, then, from the standard of morals to the motive of morals as Jesus established it, it seemed to be love, justly and fully composed of its two elements of admiring appreciation and personal gratitude.

The working of this motive we saw, first, in the play of discontent and hope which characterizes all the moral life of Christianity; second, in the use which Jesus makes of threats and punishments; third, in the relation which He establishes between forms and methods on the one hand and impulses and purposes upon the other; and, fourth, in His distinct embrace of all motive within His own person.

And last of all I tried to show how Christian morality, as the result of all that I had pointed out before, was marked supremely by the duties of sentiment, by combination of absoluteness and breadth with personal definiteness, by the effort to secure humility through aspiration, and by the courage which is born of obedience.

I know full well how lightly I have travelled over such vast, rich ground, and how much of its riches I have left ungathered. I can only hope that I have shown some thoughtful people where the riches lie, that they may go themselves and gather them.

It was in His sonship to God that the secret of the holiness of Jesus lay. His Father's business was the sum of all His life. He knew no motive except that which was summed up in the gratitude of His great prayer: "Father, I have glorified Thee on the earth: I have finished the work which Thou gavest Me to do." The model and the impulse of all duty He carried in His own filial heart, which was forever bearing witness to Him of His Father's perfectness. His incarnate days, with all their common duties held and illuminated in that high consciousness of sonship, must have been one with the eternity of the past and the eternity that was to be. Duty must have been its own revealer and its own reward. Liberty must have been sublimely consistent with the most scrupulous obedience. The doing right and the being right must have been like the sunshine and the sun. And what duty was to our Master it shall be to us just as soon as we are filled with His idea, just as soon as His spirit bears witness with our spirits that we too are the sons of God.

II.

THE INFLUENCE OF JESUS
ON THE SOCIAL LIFE OF MAN.

THE INFLUENCE OF JESUS

ON THE SOCIAL LIFE OF MAN.

A TRAVELLER in the Old World is deeply interested in seeing what are the most complete embodiments of themselves which the different struggles of human nature in thought and devotion, have left in art. I remember well the impression of contrast which I received from two when I saw them for the first time, many years ago. In one of the most rich and beautiful of European galleries hangs Raphael's greatest Madonna, called the Madonna of St. Sixtus. Among the dreary sands at the edge of the Egyptian desert, under the shadow of the Pyramids, stands the mighty Sphinx, the work of unknown hands, so calm and so eternal in its solitude that it is hard to think of it as the work of human hands at all; as true a part of the great earth, it seems, as any mountain that pierces upward from its bosom. These two suggest comparisons which are certainly not fancies. They are the two great expressions, in art, of the two religions, — the religion of the East and of the West. Fatalism and Providence they seem to mean. Both have tried to express a union of humanity with something which is its superior; but one has joined it only to the superior strength of the animal, while the other has filled it with the superior spirituality of a divine nature. One unites wisdom and power, and claims man's homage for that conjunction. The other combines wisdom and love, and says, "Worship this." The Sphinx has life in its human face written into a riddle, a puzzle, a mocking bewilderment. The Virgin's face is full of a mystery we cannot fathom, but it unfolds to us a thousand of the mysteries of life. It does not mock, but blesses us. The Sphinx oppresses us with colossal size. The Virgin is not a distortion or exaggeration, but a glorification of humanity. The Egyptian monster is alone amid its sands, to be worshipped, not loved. The Christian woman has her child clasped in her arms, enters into the societies and sympathies of men, and claims no worship except love.

It is in this last difference — the difference between the solitude of one and the companionship of the other — that we feel, I think, most distinctly how different is the Christianity of the picture from the sublime paganism of the statue. The picture is Christian, because it is so truly human. It has not lost humanity in trying to interpret Deity. It invites, entices, wins the soul of the man who studies it. It folds itself about his life with a kindred life. It wants him. It seeks him. It is not satisfied till it has found him. Then, as if it were satisfied, there seems to come a new depth in its color, a new sweetness in its celestial light.

I am to speak to you to-day of the way in which the influence of Jesus enters into the social life of man. I have been led to this remembrance of what we may almost call the constructive power in a great work of Christian art. It is positive, and finds and fastens the relationship of human souls to the Divine soul, and so of human souls to one another. As I began to write this lecture, in the midst of the Christmas days, I could not help feeling how the same idea was present in that ever-vivid scene of Bethlehem, which shines in the simple and inspired words of the first chapters of the Gospels with a clearness and a depth that the pencil of Raphael could never give. A father, a mother, and a child are there. No religion which began like that could ever lose its character. The first unit of human life, the soul, is there in the new-born personality of the childhood. But the second unit of human life, the family, is just as truly there in the familiar relation of husband and wife, and the sacred, eternal mystery of motherhood. He who would know the whole about this Jesus must learn not merely what his own soul will grow to be, but likewise what new life the presence of Jesus in the midst of it will give to this the primal typal group of human life and to all the other groups, the larger families which this one represents.

Let me define, then, in a few words, what I want to do to-day. It is to show how the idea of Jesus is the constructive power of the social life of man in all its various degrees. That idea we saw in our last lecture was the sonship of man to God, revealed in the sonship to God of Jesus

Christ himself. All that He had to show man He had first in Himself; and it was by the development in men's sight of His own gradually conscious life that He revealed to men all that they might become. If this be true, then it is by a study of the social life of Jesus, by seeing how His experience from the very beginning opened into successive relationships, and claimed for itself larger and yet larger intercourses, that we can get His true idea of how the relationships and intercourses of all men ought to be built, how that idea of the Divine Father may become the shaping and cohesive power of them all. This makes the duty that lies before us once more a Biblical study. In those old stories of the Gospels lies our material. Every one of those stories is the idea of Jesus flashed from a new side of His jewel life. All that the fatherhood of God may be to any of His children it was first and perfectly to that only-begotten Son. If we can see what He was among his fellow-men and what His life among them was to Him, we shall have the key to all the mysteries and prob'ems of our own social life.

In the first place, then, the social life of Jesus underwent the natural and human progress and change from an instinctive impulse to a deliberate and reasonable conduct. He would have been no true child and man, He would have been a human monster, if it had not been so. I think that it is a most happy sign of the healthy reality which the life of Jesus is gaining in men's thoughts in these our modern days, that this idea of the development of his consciousness, the gradual growth into the knowledge and the use of His own nature, is no longer an idea that bewilders and shocks the believer in the Lord's divinity. It is felt to be a necessary part of the belief in His humanity. Two centuries, perhaps one century, ago, I think that Christ was far less real to men than He is now. However it may have been with the last century, the century before the last was a religious age. But its religion had grown strangely impersonal. It believed doctrines far more than it believed in the Son of Man. The seventeenth century believed the divinity of Christ, but its belief in the divine Christ was weak, and the belief in the human Christ was wellnigh lost, and with this loss I cannot but feel that we must in some way connect the dislike of Christmas and its observance which then arose, and which is but just now passing entirely away. It had its local causes, which account for it, no doubt. But the whole idea of childhood, with its necessary concomitant idea of growth, was a bewilderment and almost an offence to that theology whose Christ was a mysterious and unaccountable being, a true spiritual Melchisedec, without vivid and real human associations, without age, without realized locality, a dogma, a creed, a fulfilment of prophecy, an adjustment of relations, not a man. It is because Jesus to-day is intensely real, intensely human to us, that we welcome and do not dread the truth of increase and development from babyhood to the full strength and stature of a man.

And nowhere is this clearer or more beautiful than in that feature of His life which we have to-day to study. The social life of Christ was first an instinct. The child clasped His tiny arms about His mother's neck, or laid His little hand into the strong hand of Joseph, as they walked on the long road to Egypt, with the same simple desire to utter love and to find love which is the first sign of Life akin to their own that millions of parents' hearts have leaped to recognize in their first-born. Nay, he but little understands the dignity and unity of all God's vast creation who is offended or distressed when he is told that in the Lord of Life these primal affections were of the same sort with those which make the beauty of the life of the beings which are less than man. Even the dog, the bird, the lion, know these first instincts of companionship which found their consummate exhibition upon earth when the Son of Mary clung to a human mother with a human love. That instinctive character never passed out of the relationships of Christ. When He bade the disciples go with Him to the mountain of transfiguration or to the garden of the agony, beneath every design of their enlargement or enlightenment, who does not feel beating the simple human desire for company in the supremely triumphant or supremely terrible moments of life? When He looks at His disciples, as the multitude are leaving Him, and asks them, "Will ye also go away?" or when these same disciples forsake Him and flee upon the night of trial, below the sorrow that He feels for their defection as a sign of their unworthiness, who does not hear the poor heart cry out with that same dread of being left alone which the forlorn wretch in his prison feels as the cell door clashes to between him and humanity? We must start with this instinct, and always this instinct must remain, felt like the beating heart which makes it live, underneath all the fuller understanding of itself into which the companionship of Christ, his social life, may grow. But such a growing understanding comes. As Jesus develops into manhood, the idea of His existence grows and rounds itself to clearness. By and by He is full of the consciousness that He is the Son of God, and that through His sonship this world-full of men is to learn that they are God's sons and are to be brought back to their Father. And when He had been filled with that idea, then the instinct which had already drawn Him to his brethren found its interpretation. He knew why He sought them.

It was for the self-indulgence of His own consciousness, and it was for the enlightenment of theirs. By and by, if I ask why Jesus shrinks from solitude, and craves to have John and James and Peter with him, I find myself able to say, I find myself compelled to say, something more than just that such is His healthy human instinct. I recognize that He is deliberately seeking two things there : first, the self-knowledge of His own sonship to God ; and, second, the enlightenment of these men's consciousness to know that they are the sons of God. I see the sun break in with a triumphant burst of light upon a chamber set with countless jewels, but which has thus far been wholly shut up in the dark. There is a double joy, I think, in the great heart of the sunlight as, almost with a shout that one can hear, it floods the opened chamber with itself. First, it finds new interpretation of itself, it finds itself, as it were, in the new stories of its glory which the jewels tell, as, one by one, they burn under its touch ; and, second, it feels every jewel quiver under its fiery hand with the transporting discovery of its own nature. I see a good man, long shut out from human company, come among his brethren. With a leap and burst almost like the sunshine, he casts his solitude behind him and flings himself into their sympathies and hopes. I let the explanation of it at first rest in the mere unexplained instinct of humanity; but when I come to analyze his motive to its elements, I know that it must be made up of these two impulses, the desire of self-knowledge and the desire of illuminating others, the desire of burning and the desire of shining, which are the two strong, ineradicable passions of the soul. The man goes into the multitude that he may find himself and that he may declare them to themselves. All human society which has not these impulses more or less consciously within it is but the herding of animals for the mere fear of being alone or the mere joy of being together.

All this is illustrated with great clearness in that event which has a profound interest as marking the first recorded time when Jesus ever deliberately and of His own accord sought the society of His fellow-men. He lingered behind the group into which the mere circumstances of

His life had cast Him, and for Himself He sought the venerable doctors in the Temple. What took Him there? To find Himself and to show them to themselves. The two great, everlasting human impulses, the impulse of the student seeking to know himself, and the impulse of the missionary seeking to enlighten men, — these two, which partial men call inconsistent and incompatible with one another, burned with a single flame — the first no doubt the brightest, but yet incapable of being separated from the other — in the soul of Jesus, as, among His brethren, He began to "be about His Father's business."

In general, then, the social nature of man is the provision at once for his most complete self-consciousness and for his fullest activity and efficiency. It was by losing His life in the multitude and mass of lives, in the body of the humanity to which He belonged, that Jesus at once found His own life and found the lives of the lost whom He had come to seek. At the very outset He bore witness that not in absolute singleness, not in elemental unity and perfect solitude of being, is the highest existence to be found. He recognized at once in man that multiplicity and power of relationship within the unit of humanity which makes the richness of our human life. If it be so, as we believe it is, that in the constitution of humanity we have the fairest written analogue and picture of the Divine existence, then shall we not say that the human Christ gave us, in the value which He set on human relationships, in His social thought of man, an insight into the essentialness and value of that social thought of God which we call the doctrine of the Trinity? May it not be that only by multiplicity and interior self-relationship can Divinity have the completest self-consciousness and energy? Surely, the reverent and thoughtful eye must see some such meaning when Jesus Himself makes the eternal companionship of the life of Deity the pattern and picture of the best society of the souls of earth, and breathes out to His Father these deep and wondrous words, " As thou Father art in Me and I in Thee, that they all may be one in Us."

Let us pass on now to examine in more detail the social life of Jesus as it is written in the Gospels, and to see, if we can, what suggestions come from it to throw light upon the true methods of all social living. It naturally divides itself into the three sections into which all our relations to our fellow-men fall; and in that division it will be natural for us to consider it. I shall speak first of the natural relationships of Jesus with individuals; and then of His relation to the group of disciples which was the rudimentary church; and then of His relation to His country. The purely social, the ecclesiastical, and the patriotic life demand our study.

Every now and then there are flashes of light upon the Gospel page which let us see what a bright, sunny, sympathetic life the Savior lived, — how perfectly free from harshness and asceticism was that character which, at the same time, carried a sweet and gentle seriousness and a robust earnestness with it wherever it went. "The son of man came eating and drinking, and they say, a gluttonous man and a wine-bibber, a friend of publicans and sinners." So Jesus Himself described one day the current impression that His life made upon the people of Jerusalem.

The words are like an instantaneous photograph of that far distant time. Where one's enemies find chance to taunt, one's friends almost always find occasion to be puzzled. In those words we can see friends and enemies alike busied with the strange life of Jesus, and only gradually finding out that it was they who were strange, and not He, — gradually coming first to feel and then to understand that this life of His, so bright and yet so serious, so individual and yet so social, had reached completely what their lives were only crudely struggling after. The same feeling broke forth upon another day. Jesus was supping at a "great feast" in the house of Levi, — no sumptuous Venetian banquet, such as the great master's hand has painted, but a half-barbaric scene of profuse hospitality which merely told the host's good-will, — and the Pharisees looked on and said, "Why do the disciples of John fast, and likewise the disciples of the Pharisees, but thine eat and drink?" They hated John the Baptist, but they understood him. They found him in the same region of spiritual endeavor in which they lived themselves. They recognized in him the same desire to realize individual responsibility and the seriousness of life by isolation, by surrender, by cutting off everything which by completing life should confuse it. Jesus had pushed on where they could not follow Him. He had gone into the very heart of the society where men lose their individuality to find His, and into the very centre of that world where seriousness is ordinarily lost, to find there the true solemnity of living.

For always there are these three possible stages in every advancing moral and spiritual life. There is, first, safety in simplicity; and, second, the loss of self in complication; and then, at last, the higher self-possession in a symmetrical and harmonized multiplicity. They are the stages which are represented by childhood and young manhood and middle life, in every complete career. The child, with his simple, serene, uncomplicated thought of life, seems master of himself; the young man, tossed like a helpless swimmer in the midst of the billowy world, has lost himself; the man of middle age, who has reached the profoundest faiths and principles of living, has found himself, and lives in a steady self-possession which is to the child's security like the noonday to the dawn. Now the Pharisees were children. They were afraid of life. They wanted to perpetuate childhood by keeping it out of the power of life. John Baptist's disciples, too, were children; only the difference was that their great master knew that the true childhood does not last, but turns to something greater. He sent his disciples forth into life, — the life of exposure, and so the life of true attainment, — when he pointed them to Jesus and said, " Behold the Lamb of God which taketh away the sins of the world,"— not merely stifles them and keeps them down, but "taketh them away."

Nowhere is Jesus satisfied until He himself has reached, and till He has led His disciples on towards, this third region of completed character, and made them possess themselves, not in solitude, where character would be so much easier and so much more imperfect, but in contact with the world. I know that we lose much of the beauty of His treatment, both of Himself and of His servants, when we feel about in its clear depths for conscious and definite intentions. I know that He, above all men, did what He did because He was what He was, — from a deeper necessity than any deliberate persuasion that His disciples needed this or that teaching at this or that special time. But still, as we formulate the impulses of nature into the laws of nature, and find reasons, which the winds and suns do not care themselves to know, why they should blow and shine just as we feel and see them, — reasons true, though not the truest or the deepest, — so we may dare to say about the acts of Jesus, "He must have done this act for this," if we can only keep the deeper knowledge that He did every act just as He did it because He was Jesus, and could not do it otherwise. Using such reverent liberty, I think we may love to study the way in which He opened every social event into its deeper meaning, so that the men who were in danger of losing themselves in the crowd might really find themselves, might enter into a self-possession there which they could not attain in solitude. Let us look at a few.

Jesus went one day to a marriage feast at the little town of Cana. Why did He go? I know no reason except that for which we go to where our friends are happy, — to make them know that we are glad because of their happiness. When He came there, the rooms were full of men and women, all vividly conscious that they belonged to one another. Husbands and wives, brothers and sisters, all degrees of kinship, all kinds of cousins, all feeling their common blood upon this family holiday. To Him, the grave, strong, sweet-faced man who stood among them, so familiar yet so strange, they were His Father's children. They had forgotten that. They were so absorbed in their brotherhoods that they had forgotten their Father. The miracle which Jesus did was like the opening of a window upward, so that that truth shone down upon them. They were giving one another bread and meat in token of their brotherhood. Suddenly Jesus spoke to the water in the jars, and there was wine before them, so suddenly, so mysteriously, so apart from any ministry which they were doing to each other, that they looked into one another's faces and felt divinity. They said, "Our Father must be here. We are not only brothers, we are children. Let us remember that." And each remembered it the better because he did not drink the mysterious wine alone, but saw his brethren drinking it beside him. Each found himself the child of God more easily because of the fragment of the universal family in which the wonder and awakening came to him.

Or turn again to one of the scenes of which I spoke in the last lecture. Jesus went once to supper in a ruler's house. Again the consciousness of brotherhood lay like a rich atmosphere through the great, softly lighted hall. While they are eating, behold a poor creature comes creeping in, and casts herself at the feet of the honored Guest, and begins (what other words can describe it except those dear words of the story?) to "wash His feet with her tears, and did wipe them with the hairs of her head, and kissed His feet and anointed them with the ointment." Jesus looked up, and with clear, brave, simple words told the perplexed company that she was one of them, able to love, able to trust, able to be forgiven. What then? All these are privileges and powers of childhood knowing a fatherhood above it. The guests listened; and as when a group of men, — all prosperous, all respectable, brothers to one another, — talking together, see suddenly among them one, their brother too, but poor, sick, wretched, pitiable, and then their thoughts turn back to the house where they all were children, and the father who was father to them all; as the very sight of inequality compels the simple sense of brotherhood to complete itself with the memory of fatherhood; so, when Jesus lifted this poor creature up and said, as He looked round upon the upright, reputable men, "This is your sister," the brotherhood that filled the hall warmed with the deeper memory of fatherhood, and the guests found their childhood to God in the strange society of the noblest of His sons and the most degraded of His daughters.

There was one house where Jesus went very often, — the cottage of Mary and Martha and Lazarus at Bethany. There He lived not merely a social but a domestic life, — not merely a life of society, but a life of home. In that house, brotherhood and sisterhood bloomed into such perfect flower that it has been fragrant and beautiful to all the generations. They were religious people. No doubt each of them in solitude strove after and found the fatherhood of God. But we can well imagine that when they were together it was their brotherhood and sisterhood that was most prominent. And what did Jesus do for them? Silver and gold, like His disciple, He had none; but such as He had, His own supreme consciousness, such as He was, He gave to them. One day He told the anxious elder sister that there was a "better part" in life than the most faithful work for the comfort of brother and of sister. He taught her His own lesson, that man doth not live by bread alone, but by every word that proceedeth out of the mouth of God his Father. On another solemn day He allowed the household life to feel the shock of death and to be broken, in order that He might call upon His Father and their Father to restore it by what was like to a new birth. And as the coming of a child into a household breaks open its narrowness to let in the broad thought of God, so the brotherhood and sisterhood of Bethany must have been deepened and filled with the consciousness of sonship and daughtership, whenever that boy-man — young forever with something of the perpetual youth of those who have passed through the grave and come out in the timeless life beyond — went about among them.

I turn to one scene more. Jesus was teaching one day in the Temple, doing His Father's business, and some one told Him that far off, on the outside of the crowd, His mother and His brothers were waiting to talk with Him. He paused perhaps a moment, as if pondering whether He should leave His work, and then, just, it seems to me, as if He stooped down and took hold of the human relationship which had been offered Him, and turned it over to show men its diviner side, He looked around and said, " Who are My mother and My brethren?" And then, stretching out His hand to His disciples, " These are My mother and My brethren." It was as if He said, " Motherhood and brotherhood are true and real only within the fatherhood of God. Whenever that common fatherhood is real, there is a true relationship to which the tender associations of earthly kinship are in themselves inferior. The earthly kinships are the symbol of this celestial reality. The beauty of the household is in the reality, not in the symbol. The symbol and the reality belong together. My brothers and My mother after the flesh do represent to Me, as no other beings can, the dear fatherhood of God, the relations of eternity. But sometimes the symbol must wait, lest it hinder instead of helping the reality." Therefore, Mary waited while Jesus went on and preached to those whom He claimed as "brother and sister and mother," because they were doing the will of His Father which was in heaven.

All these are illustrations. In every one of them, I take it, the meaning is the same. Jesus begins with the individual. He always does. His first and deepest touches are upon the single soul. Before all social life there is the personal consciousness and its mysterious private relations to the Father from whom it came. The father cannot teach his boy so early that God shall not have taught him first. The mother cannot drop such soft, unconscious influence into her child's soul that it shall not find the soul itself already full of the influence of God. In the individual experience man's life always begins. But there are some things of the individual life which the individual cannot get save in the company of fellow-men. There are some parts of his own true life always in his brethren's keeping, for which he must go to them. That the individual may find and be his own truest and fullest self, Jesus, his Master, leads him to his fellows. The wedding guest at Cana, the Pharisee at Levi's table, the sisters with their restored brother, the brothers of the Lord in the house of the carpenter,—all, just as soon as Jesus sanctified and blessed the society in which they lived, saw coming to them as it were out of the heart of that society a selfhood which no solitary contemplation could have gained. Each of them found his Father among his brethren,— reached God through the revelation of other human lives.

This is the fundamental truth out of which comes the regulative law of Jesus about social life. Society does not exist for itself, but for the individual; and man goes into it not to lose, but to find himself. The ancient society, the heathen society of to-day, whether in some savage island or in some fashionable parlor, is ready always to sacrifice the personal nature, the individual soul. As if society itself were an object worthy of perfecting for its own value, it overwhelms individual character and pitilessly sees lives lost in its great whirlpool. I think the great charge that Jesus, if He spoke to-day, would bring against our modern social life, our present society, as it in large part exists, would be this. He would see its impurity; He would recognize the falseness that pervades it; He would turn away from its sordidness with disappointment; but, most of all, He would miss in it that power to cultivate the personal life of the individual by the revelation of the divine side of human existence which is everywhere His ideal of social living. It is not always so. There are small groups of men gathered on such high ground that each of them becomes aware of himself, of his capacities and duties, in the association with his brethren. Especially there are friendships, the sympathetic meeting of man and man, in which each knows himself as he could not in solitude. But our ordinary life with one another, what, in the language of the world, we call *society*, has so left and lost the spontaneousness of natural impulse and so failed to attain the highest conception of itself as the family of God, it so hangs fast in the dull middle regions of conventional propriety and selfish expediency, that it becomes not the fountain, but the grave, of individuality. Men go to it to escape themselves. Men dread it, as they grow older, for younger men, because its influences seem to be fatal to original and positive character. Men flee to solitude to recruit their personality. Nowhere do we find on earth that picture of society reconstructed by the idea of Jesus, society around the throne of God, which shines out upon us from the mysterious promises of the Apocalypse; the glory of which society is to be this, — that while the souls stand in their vast choruses of hundreds of thousands, and all chant the same anthems and all work together in the same transcendent duties, yet each bears the sacred name written on the flesh of his own forehead, and carries in his hand a white stone, on which is written a new name which no man knoweth saving he that receiveth it. It is individuality emphasized by company, and not lost in it, because the atmosphere in which the company is met is the idea of Jesus, which is the fatherhood of God.

And here we come where we can understand some other things which the great Teacher said, which, if they stood alone, would puzzle us hopelessly. Here He is, in His mountain sermon, telling of what is to be the issue of His work. It is almost as if He spoke in reverie. He hardly seems to be speaking to the people, or to be conscious of them. He seems to be reading for the first time a page of the future which has never opened to Him before; or to be rereading one which, however often He may read it, is forever new and wonderful. "Think not that I am come to send peace on the earth," He says; "I came not to send peace, but a sword. For I am come to set a man at variance against his father, and the daughter against her mother, and the daughter-in-law against her mother-in-law: and a man's foes shall be they of his own household." And at another time, when He looked around, and saw a superficial multitude following Him, He seemed seized with that desire which many a true man has felt, to test and sift the allegiance that seemed to be gathering only too easily. He paused and turned, and stopped the crowd that was pursuing Him, and He cried out across their heads, so that the farthest heard Him, "If any man come to Me and hate not his father and mother and wife and children and brethren and sisters, he cannot be My disciple." There is almost defiance in the words. But they seem to me to be like so many words of Jesus which we cannot understand if we think of Him only as a teacher, only as a giver of lessons to men whom He counted His pupils. We must think of Jesus as a soul, undergoing experiences, living a life all through those years, or else the Gospels are a very dead and barren book. And if we have known what it is to look forward and see, with terror which yet is glorified by hope, that the great purpose on which our heart is set is to be won only by first casting it, with seeming recklessness, away,— if, for instance, we have seen that we must lay the foundations of a boy's true faith upon the very ruins of what he has been calling his creed ; if the reformer, full of the visions of a bright, free, happy land, knows often that he must take the firebrand and set the land on fire before he can begin his work ; if every one of us has had to disturb the unreal quiet of what called itself a friendship in order that we might be deeply and truly a friend to some heart which he coveted,— if all these are familiar things, then we can understand how the Rebuilder of human life about the fatherhood of God dwelt with pathetic certainty upon the destruction that must come before that construction could begin. The more intensely He knew the preciousness of the end, the more necessary and the more terrible became the seeming sacrifice of that end over which He must go to reach it. The more He gloried, with His heart full of the memories of heaven, in the prospect of the re-established family of God, where each child should find his own distinctive childhood in the common filial life of all, so much the more He saw with sadness, but with certainty, that the merely human groupings of men, in which each man lost his own true self among his brethren, must be broken up. The more He longed to see the Temple full of consecrated worshippers, the more ruthlessly He drove out the barterers and hucksters who had monopolized its courts.

The key, then, to all Christ's treatment of man's social life lies here, — in the constant desire to foster the consciousness of divine sonship by intercourse with those who are fellow-sons of the same Father. And here we see what is meant by the constant alternation, the effort after balance, as it were, between society and solitude, first in the life of Jesus himself, and then in the life which He enjoined on His disciples. Think over some of the purely solitary moments which Jesus passed. No sooner was His work fairly begun, no sooner was He completely consecrated to it, than the Spirit, His Spirit, took Him away from the company of His home, and the solitude of the Temptation followed. The need of realizing

Himself had come. He must struggle into the knowledge of what it meant to be in the world. He must meet the devil of doubt and of despair. It is a most mysterious event, but its mystery is of that sort which becomes more and more mysterious to us, not because it is so unlike, but because it is so like, what goes on in our own careers. That is always the most wonderful sort of mystery. Jesus, there in the desert, shakes His life free, as it were, from the shell of childhood, and thereby, for the first time, takes possession of the perfectly childlike soul. He is a man, and the secret which manhood whispers into His ear in that moment of initiation, — a secret not new and yet forever new, because it is infinite, — is simply that God is His Father. Care, obedience, trust, the holding back of the life until the Father bids it go, the sending forth of the life wherever the Father demands it, — these, which are the elements of conscious childhood, Jesus took up there in the desert. That totality of life, that unity of it in a single conception and a single use, which often afterwards came so grandly from His lips, — it must have been there in the desert that He came to know it first.

All that was done in solitude. And then, when the idea is there, when the core and centre of life has been set, He comes down, and instantly He draws near to men and draws men to Him. About that core, both for its own satisfaction and safety and for the blessing of the lives He summons, He must group the souls into a society. He sees Simon Peter and Andrew, and they are no sooner with Him than James and John are beckoned with a bright gesture or challenged with a ringing word from their half-mended nets; and then, with them around Him, He plunges into populous Galilee, and all its villages begin to know His face and watch for His coming, and make their contribution to His company. Solitude makes the consciousness; society develops, multiplies, and confirms it. That which would have remained only a quality in Him, if He had stayed in the desert, becomes a life when He goes forth into the world. What Goethe wisely says of all men does not lose its truth when we are thinking of the Son of Man: "A talent shapes itself in stillness, but a character in the tumult of the world." This is Christ's balance between solitude and society.

Each makes the other necessary. With us they often lose this value, because they are not set in any relation to each other. Solitude is barren, and so society is frivolous. Solitude creates no consciousness for society to ripen. Solitude is like an unfertile seed, and society is like an unplanted ground. Each craves the other, not because it wants its complement, but because it is tired of itself and longs to change.

I think there is something exquisitely beautiful in the unerring play of this balance in the life of Jesus. Not more surely does the night open into day than solitude fulfils itself with company. Once and again He goes apart into a mountain and prays by Himself all night. No one is there but Him and God. The silence is like heaven about Him. But as the morning comes a new need certainly comes with it. No longer loneliness, but company; not solitude, but voices; and so the earliest light finds Him among the crowd of His disciples choosing His twelve apostles, or walking across the boisterous waters of Gennesaret to join His toiling servants in their boat. Everybody must have felt how the two needs tremble in response to one another in the intense atmosphere of that vivid night before His crucifixion. It seems as if He took great deep draughts of the idea of His life, of the fatherhood of His Father, as if it entered by great waves into His soul, and as if each wave so overwhelmed the soul it filled that He needed to reassure and recover Himself in the familiar company of His disciples. First there is the long conversation of the Supper. Then comes the terrible solitude of the Garden of Gethsemane. Again and again the Sufferer comes wandering back to where the tired and unconscious men are lying. It is as one who was passing through some deep experience might go into the chamber where a child was sleeping and find relief when the burden of the solitary crisis was too great to bear. Then, as the Lord's career sweeps more and more into that channel where it must run alone, where none can share it, how, still, the craving for society seems to beat responsive to every new throb of suffering! He turns and looks at Peter; He would almost open his heart to Pilate; He looks back and tells the women who follow him to Calvary about the future of the beloved land that murdered Him; and at last, even upon the cross, He has mercy to give to the robber at His side, and care still for His mother and the disciple whom He loved. Every moment of deepening communion with His Father has its corresponding moment of sympathy with His brother men. The two halves of the great heart die together as they have lived together. The balance trembles more and more lightly as the life beats lower, but it trembles still even to the last, and Jesus ceases to love only when He ceases to live.

And this same poise and mutual supply which was between society and solitude in the life of Jesus Himself He was always trying to establish in the lives of those whom He taught. One day He cured a man of lunacy. It was a deep mystery to the poor creature. He wanted to go with Jesus, to leave his house and friends and country, to hide his life under the shelter of this power of God, and to study it forever. Jesus quietly lays the finger of His authority upon the other scale and says, "Go home to thy friends."

Another day He raises a dead girl to life, and, just as the glad father and mother and all the eager friends are rushing forth into the street to tell their joy and wonder, He lifts his finger and says, "See that no man knows it!" And so it is always with the separate scholars of His school. Peter wants to stay upon the mountain of transfiguration, and his Master leads him down among the needs of men, to where the poor boy with the unclean spirit is foaming and raving at the mountain's foot. Nicodemus sits with Him in the midnight chamber. The next time we see him he is saying a timid word for the Lord in the Sanhedrim. The woman of Sychar fulfils the quiet conversation at the well by the impetuous seeking of the men whom she knew in the city, that they might be the sharers of her joy. Everywhere the solitary completes itself in the social. Solitude shapes and colors the precious forms of character which then the furnace of society burns to solidity and brilliancy and permanence.

I am often struck by seeing how the loftiness of the life of Jesus altogether escaped the perplexity of many of the questions with which our lives are troubled, as the eagle flying through the sky is not worried how to cross the rivers. We debate whether self-culture or our brethren's service is the true purpose of our life. We vacillate aimlessly. Now we shut ourselves up and meditate and try to grow. Now we rush forth and make the wide world ring with what we call our work. The two so often have no connection with each other. We are so apt to live two lives. But Jesus knows but one. All culture of His soul is part of our salvation. All doing of His work is ripening His nature. Jesus in the still night far off upon a solitary hill-top, Jesus in broad daylight dragged by a hooting mob from Pilate's judgment-seat to Calvary, both of them are Jesus saving the world; both of them are Jesus living His life. And not until our brawling ceases and the champion of each side of the question rounds his truth with his adversary's truth which he has been denouncing, not until the apostle of self-culture knows that no man can come to his best by selfishness, and the apostle of usefulness knows that no man can do much for other men who is not much himself, — not until then shall men have fairly started on the broad road to the completeness of God their Father in the footsteps of the Son of Man.

It remains only to speak of one or two of the special exhibitions of the social life of Jesus in illustration of what I have been saying. One of the most interesting is His treatment of men in classes. It is always saved from the extravagance and grotesqueness into which the emphasis of class lines tends to run by the strong value of the individual life which lay at the bottom of His consciousness. Indeed, I think that as one reads that interesting story of how the various groups of men came up to John the Baptist and received his teaching about their special duties, first "the people," then "the publicans," and then "the soldiers," one feels how different that is from anything in the life of Jesus. He deals, indeed, with the great classes into which men were divided in His time. He was known as the friend of publicans. He cried aloud before the multitude, " Woe unto you, Scribes and Pharisees," but He was no partisan of wealth nor any more of poverty; whoever listened to Him could not help feeling that in His view the class was good or bad only as it made the individual good or bad, and that no class condition could overrule the essential condition of the personal souls within it. Here is where all party spirit shows its viciousness. Here is where all socialism shows its weakness. Here is where all the weak idolatry of organic methods fails. It loses sight of the final unit in its watch over some of the accidental and temporary combinations of mankind. The final unit is the man. And that unit of value was never out of the soul of Jesus. After the day when He told them the story which they never could forget, of how there was a man with a hundred sheep and how one of them wandered from the flock and got astray among the hills, and of how the shepherd left all the rest and went and found that one and came down out of the hills singing, with the rescued sheep across his shoulders, — after that keynote of the preciousness of the individual had been struck, it never ceased to be heard through everything that Jesus said and did. When He sat at rich men's tables His proud hosts knew that it was not because they were rich but because they were men that He had come to them. When He entered poor men's huts they knew that it was not their poverty but their manhood that He honored. And that which, on the whole, has kept Christianity from becoming the religion of any class as against other classes, that which has always made it able, just when it seemed on the point of lending itself to such monopoly, to break out of the grasp of those who would put it to such partisan and partial use, has been the healthy and ineradicable individualism which is at its heart. Men cry to-day, "Christianity is the religion of the rich and comfortable," and while they speak their cry is drowned in the rush of the poor, the hungry, and the wretched to some common men's revival. They cry again. "The Christian belief belongs to the ignorant," and lo, the wisest thought of the world comes back again as it is ever coming to the mystery of Christ and of His treatment of the soul of man. It is not that they have mistaken the class to which they should assign the Christian faith.

Their mistake has been in giving it to any class. It belongs to the individual. It always has its eye fastened on him. One of the noblest functions of Christianity in the world is to lie behind the class crystallizations of mankind, like a solvent into which they shall return and blend with one another, to crystallize, no doubt, again, but always to be reminded that the classes into which they crystallize are lesser facts than the manhood into which they are repeatedly dissolved.

We must put here, no doubt, the deep interest with which Jesus looked always at the young. He was talking of deep and difficult things, and through the crowd there came a little company of women bringing their children for Him to bless. Instantly He turned aside from the grown men and women, and, waving His disciples' interference back, His hands were on the little wondering creatures' heads. And when a young man came with a puzzled question, the teller of the story years afterwards remembered the look which was in the eyes of Jesus as He answered him. "Jesus beholding him loved him," Mark writes. In both these stories, and perhaps still more in the way in which He surrounded Himself with that garland of vigor and enthusiasm, the cluster of young men whom He called His disciples, everywhere there is the value set on youth. And youth is the period of individual life, of individual hope. Class life has not begun. The child of the king and the child of the beggar will play together if no older wisdom or folly interferes. Nay, the queen who will not let the beggar's fingers touch her robe will take the beggar's baby in her arms and clasp it to her bosom. He who touches a child of any class touches, as it were, the undivided humanity, and his touch may be felt anywhere through all its classifications. He who speaks to the infant speaks to mankind behind the Babel of its divisions. No wonder that Socrates was accused at Athens that he corrupted the youth. No wonder that Jesus said of little children, "Of such is the kingdom of Heaven."

Another interesting point in the social life of Jesus is His courtesy. There is perhaps, no part of our life that is so unreal and unsatisfactory, none of which we find it so hard to give an account to ourselves, as the courtesy which we pay to one another. And there is none which, in the life of Jesus, is more thoroughly satisfactory and perfect. I find the secret of it in the clear perception and value of the personal life behind the class condition of which we have just been speaking. True courtesy gets its essence from honor of the individual, while it gets its special form from consideration of the class condition. I may be just as courteous to the beggar as to the king, but I do not treat them both alike. Now, when Jesus met the woman of Samaria at the well He honored her; He valued and reverenced her soul. When He met Pontius Pilate, He honored him. When He dealt day after day with the ripening treachery of Judas Iscariot, He honored him. When He found John the Baptist making the door ready through which He was to enter on His work, He honored him. The spiritual nature, the special humanity, of each of them seemed to Him, not in any mere fiction but in simple truth, to be a beautiful and precious thing. His honor for that was the soul of His courteousness. And then the special words He said, whether of sympathy or of rebuke, might be just what the special occasion bade them be. Different as they were, they were all courteous alike because of this personal honor and value that filled them all. There is no complete courtesy that has not such a soul and such a body, — a soul of honor for the individual, living in and uttering itself through the intelligent recognition of the class condition.

Or, look at the way in which this principle governs all the treatment by Jesus of the hard question of privilege. Privilege, which is a pervading, obstinate fact in the world, becomes an exasperating fact from the crude confusion of personal nature with official life or accidental circumstances. Let the two be finely and constantly discriminated, and privilege loses the largest part of its obnoxiousness, — loses all its obnoxiousness for the best and noblest men. Perhaps this discrimination was never more finely or clearly made than on that day when, after one of the discussions with the rulers of the people, in which they had tried to browbeat Him with the authority of their position, Jesus quietly turned to the multitude and His disciples and said to them, " The Scribes and the Pharisees sit in Moses' seat. All therefore whatsoever they bid you observe, that observe and do, but do not ye after their works." I can easily conceive of how the scales may have dropped from the eyes of some ingenuous Jew as he listened to those words. Behold, it was possible to own and recognize these men's position, and yet not be obliged to call them good when they were bad, or great when they were little. Behold, one might keep his own intellect and conscience true, and yet not seize the sword to destroy all present social order. Behold, one might obey present authority, and yet be expectant of the coming day when only the best should rule. To the listener who heard all that in the words of Jesus, the privilege of the Scribes and Pharisees was no longer an exasperation. His hate and envy of them turned to pity. There might be other men not morally within the sound of the Lord's voice, who would still be jealous of the soft cushions and the pompous words of the men who sat in Moses's seat; but they were only Scribes and Pharisees out of office emulating the vices of the Scribes and Pharisees who happened to be in.

As Jesus in His earthly life was always feeding His human nature out of the Divine nature on which it rested in mysterious unity, so were His special judgments always drawing largeness and truth from the simple and eternal principles which lay below them in His consciousness. This was the secret both of His boldness and His prudence. Indeed, I think that we can hardly speak of Jesus as either bold or prudent in the way in which we speak of other men. The region of principles, of absolute righteousness and truth, lies above the consciousness of prudence and of boldness; and it was in that region that He lived and moved. An illustration of this is found in His dealing with yet another of the perplexing questions of men's social life. They brought to Him, one morning in the Temple, the poor shame-stricken creature whom they had arrested in adultery. And Jesus, no doubt seeing first that He had touched her conscience, bade her go free and live a better life, in a way that must have seemed, even to thoughtful and sympathetic Jews, to open the door to dangerous license in family life and personal chastity. Then, when perhaps this impression was still fresh in the minds of men, there came another morning. Jesus was in Judea again. And one day His old enemies, the Pharisees, remembering, perhaps, what He had said to the wretched woman, began to ask Him about marriage and divorce. And then Jesus amazed them with the lofty stringency of His ideas. He went back beyond Moses. What Moses had allowed He would allow no longer. "Whosoever shall put away his wife, except it be for fornication, and shall marry another," He declares, "committeth adultery." But along with His decree comes the deep principle on which it is based, — "Have ye not read that He which made them at the beginning made them male and female?" It all goes back to the creation. It is part of the birthright of man from the hand of his Father, this right of the wife to the husband and of the husband to the wife. It is no mere arrangement for the good order of society. It is in the very nature of the children of God. It is in this fundamentalness of its character that the secret of His large treatment of it lay. If it had been an arbitrary rule of society, it could not have been trifled with. A single indulgence would have scattered it forever. But an essential principle has flexibility which an arbitrary rule cannot have. A mere rule-maker can have no personal considerations. But God, in whom all principles reside, from whom they all proceed, finds room for personal discrimination and education within the application of His principles. It is the depth of His government that makes the specialness of His government. It is because His government comes out of the profoundest secrets of His character, that it is able to adapt itself to all the individual peculiarities of our lives. Who can say how this truth may affect that seeming conflict between the law of God and the mercy of God which has driven men to shape for themselves such strange and artificial doctrines of atonement? And it is in the wonderful combination of the vast and transcendental with the minute and the familiar in Him who was both "conceived of the Holy Ghost" and also "born of the Virgin Mary," that the fitness of the Savior not merely for the rescue of the soul, but for the salvation of society, is found.

I have dwelt so very long upon the influence of Jesus upon the general social life of man, that not many moments are left to speak of His life in the Church and in the State, which were parts of the subject that I undertook to treat. But not many moments are needed for the little that I want to say on each. I am not called upon to write an ecclesiastical or a political treatise. I only want to try to see, according to the simple picture which the Gospel gives us, how these two great organisms which have so filled history with their power, the Church and the State, looked in the eyes and stood forth in the words of the deep, transparent man of Judea and Galilee whose influence we have been endeavoring to feel.

Of the Church of Jesus I think we never

cease to be surprised when we see, as we read the Gospels with eyes out of which the mist of ecclesiastical history has been wiped, how naturally and simply and artlessly it was the expression of the life of Jesus. I wish that I could tell the story with as entire an absence of the institutional and magical and artificial air which the subsequent centuries have breathed around it as it has while it lies shining there in that unconscious and immortal story.

The great French writer who has told the story of the life of Jesus has at least revived for us one picture which we had almost lost behind the curtaining mists of the long Christian history. He has shown us the Master walking with His group of disciples along the borders of Gennesaret, now lingering in a little village, now traversing a field of corn, now pausing on the high bluff beyond Capernaum that overlooks the lake, now sitting in the boat and talking to His friends while they were fishing. A curious picture the Frenchman has made out of the scene. It is partly an idyl of careless peasants, partly a conclave of conspirators, partly a symposium of philosophers. It is half Arcadia and half the Agora of Athens. But through all the confused conception this at least is kept, — a clear, fresh sense of personal companionship, of a group gathered and held about a personal centre, and gradually becoming fired with the idea with which that central life was burning, until, regenerated by that idea itself, the group became the regenerating power of the world. If we look simply at the transparent story of the Gospels, that picture gives us, beyond all doubt, the cradle, the cell-life, of the Christian Church. The history is full of human nature. The opening life of Jesus was full of His consciousness that He was the Son of God. The ambition of which His soul was full was the desire to let men know that they, too, were the sons of God, and to rescue them into the full enjoyment of their sonship. That desire gave to the young man's opening life a relationship to all humanity. All these men about Him were His unconscious brethren, the unconscious children of the Father in whose life all His life was bound up. I can think of the boy Jesus, as this consciousness grew in Him, going from day to day with deepening awe about the streets of the Galilean village which was His world. The men who laid their hands upon His head, the women who chattered to Him with their motherly good-will, the boys and girls He played with, — it was dawning upon Him that these were all children of His Father. But by and by, out of the multitude, began to gather about Him those in whom this consciousness of His awoke some kindred consciousness. A young man here, a woman there, sometimes a very child, with a child's insight and a child's strange outlook, — all these began to find themselves interpreted in Him. Their deepest questions of their own life found some answer in what they saw Him being every day. The process was miraculous, was a wonder, not in its kind, but in its degree, — in the depth to which it opened their souls and filled their doubts with light. First came the mere attraction of His presence and His person. Then it was found that this attraction had its source in a nature which they gradually came to know. Then the sight of this nature became a revelation of their own possibilities; a new life for themselves, like His life, opened to them. Then there gradually shone out from this revelation its central idea, that which made their possibility possible, that in whose full realization their possibility should be perfectly attained. They were the sons of God; and then every kindness, every self-sacrifice, every devotion of His life with them, softened their lives more deeply with love, for the more and more complete reception of this transforming idea into their heart of hearts. This little group of people, who had more or less thoroughly learned what Jesus was revealing every day, made up the slowly compacted company of the disciples. It seemed as if it were going to stop there, perhaps. If it had, there would have been only another sect added to the many sects of religionists that filled the world. But what came next? One morning, after Jesus had been praying on a mountain by Himself all night, as soon as it was day, "He called unto Him His disciples, and of them He chose twelve whom also He named apostles." Out of the heart of the discipleship comes the apostleship. Out of the centre of the learning comes the transmission. The inward tendency reacts into the outward tendency. The idea of Jesus, which has been revealing itself to a few and enshrining itself in their experience, reclaims its essential universalness; and the best of the learners are the first to be sent forth into the world, which is the true partner in all that they have found. Jesus says to the most earnest of them all, "I will give unto thee the key of the kingdom of heaven." He touches their experience, and bids them remember all that they have learned. "Ye are witnesses of these things," He declares. Some outward force gave sign of the idea they carried. "He gave them power over unclean spirits." All these things surrounded them with certain personal importance. But after all it was only the necessary pulsing forth of that which had been gathered inward for the outward spring. It was He that really went forth, and His going forth was the going forth of the Father whose revelation He was. "He that receiveth you receiveth Me, and He that receiveth Me receiveth Him that sent Me."

It is interesting to see how deep this relationship between discipleship and apostleship lies. It bears witness at once that the influence of Jesus is based upon and fed from a personal idea, and also that it belongs to all the world. By and by the outgoing Christian life began to draw in upon itself again. The dogmatic ages came. The apostles were again disciples. Then, once again, there came the expansive impulse. The later missionary work began. The newly elaborated doctrine, the deepened knowledge of God the Father in Christ the Son, reached out and craved to fill the world. It is the history of all life, this history of the Christian Church. The knowing of Jesus and the telling of Jesus minister to and succeed each other, — the scholar life and the missionary life, the inward and the outward movement, the systole and diastole of the Great Heart which beats eternally with the idea of Jesus.

Let us dwell with what interest and delight we will upon the rich history of the Church which has come since, the germ and essence of it all is in that body of disciples bound to each other by the revelation of their human sonship to the Father. It is a family picture. The Lord's Supper realized in the simplest way as the Father's table is its transparent sacrament. I would let a man forget, or never know, all about councils and bishops, all about corruptions and reformations, all about creeds and confessions. If he kept that picture, he would know the open secret of the Christian Church. He would keep these truths which are the great saving truths of ecclesiastical history, again and again submerged in the waves of angry times, but forever reappearing in their power, — the truth that the ministry of the Church is not distinct from and above the Church, but is only the Church itself in its utterance, doing and saying representatively what all the Church in all its membership has the right and the duty to say and do; and the truth that, as an elect body, the Church is but the type of the complete humanity, — elect, not that it may be saved out of the world, but that the world may be saved by its witness and specimen of what the whole world is in its idea. It is the sons of the Father who have learned their sonship through the Son crying to all the family of God, and bearing witness that to be a son of man is to be a child of the Almighty.

The church spire is nothing, after all, but the elevated and prolonged house-roof. And so the battlemented city wall is but the enlargement and solidification of the simple fence that encloses the familiar homestead. If the idea of Jesus is the constructive power of the Christian Church, it lies no less at the heart of the whole conception of the State as He conceived it. Jesus was a patriot. That sentiment which makes so much of the poetry of the earth — the love of men for their native land — was very strong in His bosom. With our modern, half-personal, unlocalized ideas of Jesus, it must always be striking — sometimes it is startling — to remember that there was one little district of a few miles square upon the surface of this earth which was known as " His own country." That little group of hills with the quiet valleys among them which lies between Nazareth and the Sea of Tiberias He loved as we love the streets or farms where we were born. And not very far off to the southward lay the great city of His race, where His feet never seemed to enter except solemnly, and over which He wept with a lamentation that is the type and pattern of every sincerest patriot's most loving and unselfish sorrow for his sinful land. And the great indignation with which Jesus lashes the Scribes and Pharisees has its primary meaning in that same passionate remonstrance which the heart of every patriot utters when the land he loves is so ruled by bad hands that he cannot give his love free utterance in approbation and support, but is compelled, perhaps, to work against his country because he must work for righteousness. No one who reads the Gospels can miss these simple, recognizable signs of the true patriotism of Jesus. But why is it that His patriotism is a part of His life to which we least often turn ? It is not only that He lived a larger life and did a larger work, which has far outreached the Jewish people and touched us with its influence. There is something in the quality of His patriotism which is peculiar, which separates it from the patriotism of the Athenian or the Roman. What is that quality? It is the constant predominance of the sonship to God over the sonship to David in his consciousness, making him always eager for the land of David, because of the interests of God which it enshrined. This is a distinct and definite quality when it appears in a man's patriotism. It makes his patriotism fine and lofty above the measure of the common patriotic feeling of mankind. It makes the patriot's relation to his land very like the man's relation to his body. The man loves his body. He works for it by natural impulse. He is not always thinking of the soul which the body contains, and which gives to it its value. And yet it always is the soul which makes the body worthy of his care and work. The body without the soul — the poor dead corpse, or the beautiful or powerful structure of an idiot — is dreadful. No man can work with healthy joy for them. And so it is, as Jesus reveals and illustrates it to us, with reference to a man's relation to his country. A true man's patriotic impulse is spontaneous. It springs up without thought. No conscious calculation makes me love the hills and valleys, the streets and houses, of the land where I was born. But yet, unless I know of something underneath all this, I am not satisfied. My patriotism lives and flutters as a sentiment unless I know that the land I love is really making, by its constant life, a contribution to the righteousness and progress of the world. When I know that, then I set my patriotic impulse free to act. My land becomes to me merely the special spot where I am placed to labor for the universal spiritual benefit of man. Then the old Psalmist's words become real to me; and as I live my life of citizen or public officer, as I take my office or cast my vote or pay my tax, I say with David, "Because of the house of the Lord our God, I will seek to do thee good." Such was the perpetual, self-limited character of the love of Jesus for His native land.

I know that here is the essence of what most men, as they look at history, are apt to dread to-day, — of a theocracy, of a religious State and of a State religion. If this which I have said be true, — if the State and its machineries be valuable to the Christian patriot, as His State was valuable to Jesus, because of the spiritual interests which they enshrine, because of the family life of man with God which they represent, — then why should he not ask that the State should manifest its spiritual function to the fullest degree by becoming distinctively and openly the minister of Christ? Why should he not ask that Christianity, as he conceives it and as it seems to him to be unspeakably important, should be taught in the State schools? Nay, why should he not ask that only men distinctively and positively Christian in belief and life should be intrusted with the conduct of the nation? How can he live, how can he be a patriot, in any land which is as purely secular in its administration as all our lands are growing more and more to be? It is an urgent question. We can only find its answer, I think, in two considerations which no man can ignore. One is that the ideas and methods of spiritual men, and even of Christian men, are so divergent from one another that it is only on the broadest basis of the most general purposes of spiritual life that they can meet,

— not in their special methods or their special creeds, but only in the desire and assertion of righteousness and truth to which all their methods and their creeds belong. The other consideration is that, even were all spiritual men at one, they still might doubt whether it would be well to make the government of their land the agent and maintainer of their faith. Any machinery of government which men have yet devised is too coarse and clumsy for so delicate a task as the inculcation and encouragement of faith. Government works by compulsion; faith, by inspirations. Government lays its hand on actions; faith nestles into unseen affections. Government estimates appearances; faith looks only at realities. And so government, though all the land were unanimously and harmoniously Christian, would still be a poor minister of Christianity. These are the considerations which make the Christian man consent to live in a State whose chosen policy is secular, and yet lets him feel that there are unowned spiritual influences and powers in her to which he may rejoice to lend his aid.

Let these considerations pass away, let all the spiritual desire and aspiration of the land be fused into a perfect unanimity of thought and action, and let some new finer machinery of governmental action be devised or developed which shall be capable of spiritual uses; and then theocracy, a religious State, a State religion, a national creed, a Christian public education, a divine responsibility in every officer, — all these would be not merely conceivable, they would be the only methods which the Christianized State could think of for a moment. There could be nothing secular in such a heavenly community as that. Only it would be altered utterly from what we see now. It would be the New Jerusalem for which we hope, and not the old earthly city which we know so well. At present we can only keep it constantly before our eyes and always proclaim it as the true ideal. We can, and I think we ought to, earnestly assert, when men praise it most loudly, that secularism, however we may accept it cheerfully, as the only expedient for the present time, is not the highest nor the eternal type of government. We may strive, by that devotion to the spiritual element in national life which even pure secularity of public methods still leaves possible, to hasten the day, which must come if Christ be what we know He is, when the idea of Jesus shall be the shaping and moving power of the Christian State; and among the happy sons of God the Son of God shall evidently reign, as the old phrase describes, "King of nations as King of saints."

I must not even stop to gather into a summary what I have said to-night. I have spoken of the principles which underlay and gave form and color to the whole social life which Jesus lived; and then specially His life with His disciples and His life with His nation. Those principles were always the same. Jesus the Friend, the Teacher, the Patriot, is always first Jesus the Son of God.

The social influence of Jesus all issues from the fatherhood of God which He reveals, and into which He claims God's children. By it the family, the Church, the State, exist. It is the power of construction and reform and education

As it is realized in each, the life of each becomes exalted and inspired. It makes all history divine. And even the world that is not yet becomes intelligible when we can look through the glowing window of the revelation and see the idea of Jesus still the constructive power of the society of heaven. "I looked," says John, "and lo! a Lamb stood on Mount Zion, and with Him an hundred and forty and four thousand having His Father's name written in their foreheads."

III.

THE INFLUENCE OF JESUS
ON THE EMOTIONAL LIFE OF MAN

THE INFLUENCE OF JESUS

ON THE EMOTIONAL LIFE OF MAN.

WE say that life is made up of joy and pain. But it is not really so. At least, when we speak in those words, we are talking of life only in its most superficial sense. Joy and pain are the expressions of life, but not life itself, not its true substance. Far down beneath them both lie the real processes of which they try to tell the tale. And even the tale they try to tell they cannot tell with certainty. The same essential life which makes one man happy makes another man sad. And so even as symptoms they perpetually mislead us. If I am really trying to get at the quality of a man's living, it means very little to me at first to know that he is a happy man. I must know a great deal more about him before I can make any use of the fact that he is happy. And when we are trying to test not the quality of another man's life but the quality of our own, all of us who are thoughtful discover very early that happiness or unhappiness may mean very much or very little, that there is a consciousness underneath sorrow and joy into which we must penetrate, in which we must live, before we can know our true lives.

And yet it is by joy and pain that lives mostly communicate with one another. The man who lacks emotion lacks expression. That which is in him remains within him, and he cannot utter it or make it influential. And on the other hand the man who lacks emotion lacks receptiveness. That which other men are, if it does not make him glad or sorry, if it gives him neither joy nor pain, does not become his. The emotion of lives is the magnetism that they emit, something closely associated with their substance and yet distinct from it, in which they communicate with one another. There is a condition conceivable in which the emotions should be so delicately and perfectly true to the quality of the lives from which they issue that they should furnish a perfect medium of communication. That would be a state of existence in which truth and goodness should inevitably shine forth in gladness from the man who was true and good, and should instantly be answered in gladness from every other man on whom they struck. The poet sings, —

> "Serene shall be our days, and bright
> And happy shall our nature be,
> When love is an unerring light,
> And joy its own security."

The prophecy declares itself not yet fulfilled. It is a noble, truthful condition for which we are waiting. Until it comes he who would find life must look behind joy and sorrow, and, while He questions them, can never let their answers pass unchallenged, must always cross-question and examine them, and see what this especial joy or sorrow means.

I am to speak to-day about the influence of Jesus through joy and sorrow, — the way, that is, in which the life that was in Him came forth from Him through His evident happiness and suffering, and entered into other men through the happiness and suffering that He awoke in them. It is the study of a subtle history, crowded with pathetic interest, which is going on through all these years of the Gospels. As I took up the subject it seemed to me to be necessary that I should say first of all what I have said, that both in Jesus and in those who come under His influence there is something behind the suffering and happiness in which they meet each other, and that the happiness and suffering are but the light or the aroma which come from the life behind. "Can any connection be traced between the chemical nature of a substance, or the conditions under which it burns, and the nature of the light which it emits?" That is the statement of one of the most interesting problems which natural science has met in this day of its many triumphs, the problem whose study has led on to the spectrum analysis and all its wonders. Can any true connection be reliably traced between the way that a man lives and the joy or sorrow that his life emits? That is the corresponding question in moral science for which no man has yet devised its spectroscope, but which, as it finds its solution more and more, must deepen a hundred-fold the intercourse of man with man and man's understanding of himself.

What, then, was it that lay behind the phenomena of pleasure and pain in Jesus? First of all, no doubt, experience, the simple doing of acts and undergoing of contacts, without regard to the emotions they produced. It is a striking fact that many of the words which, in long use of them, have become exclusively appropriated to *pain* originally belonged simply to *experience* without reference to whether it brought distress or pleasure. The old Greek and Latin words from which our words for suffering come simply meant "to undergo," and were used of the contact with happy as well as with unhappy things. It was to touch and be touched by the furniture of the great crowded world. And even our English words which are stained all through with the associations of pain, the very word "suffering" itself, and "patience" and "submission" and that hard word "bear,"—they all essentially mean nothing but experience. It is something taken on the back and carried, but that may be either a burden under which the bent back groans, or an inspiration and delight under which the shoulders leap and grow buoyant as the proud mother's arms do, when she carries her first-born child. Is it not a sign that human misery overweighs human joy, or at least a sign that men have come to think that there is far more of pain than of happiness to be suffered in the world, that the words of experience have come to be words of sadness, as if the touch of life must wound us all and make us sore? At any rate, the history of such words bears witness that there is a conception of experience back of pain and pleasure, in a region where the conception of them has not yet been born, that the life, which shows itself in enjoyment or distress, consists in the actions and contacts out of which the enjoyment or distress proceeds. And so our first step is to trace the real influential life of Jesus back into the actual experiences of His life. It is not essentially because He was happy or was sad that He has such power over men to-day. It is because of what He did.

It is because of His part in our human lot and the way in which He bore that part. If He had borne pain somewhere else, in some region of transcendental experience which we could not understand, whatever mysterious power might have been attributed to that pain in influencing the currents of the universe and its government, it never could have come to any direct influence upon the hearts and lives of men. And on the other hand, if it had been possible for Him to live our life and share our lot completely and yet have known no pain, have passed in sunny joy from Bethlehem to Olivet, His life would still have been the influential power of the world. That was not possible. To live a life like His in such a world as ours, by a deep inevitable necessity involved the pain. The cross was the predestined seal on that experience. But yet the experience is separable from the pain, and it was in the experience, not in the pain, that the true life abode.

This is the first step backward. But we cannot rest here. The mere experiences which make up any man's career cannot really constitute his life. They are too incoherent. Our histories are not our lives. The idea of life is unity. Experiences are manifold. Underneath their superficial variety they must find unity in some controlling law. They have no character save what they get from it; and without character there is no true life. The next step back, then, in the true life of Jesus is to the law which lies behind the experiences, in which must rest the reason and the meaning of His going hither and thither and meeting this and that man,— now up to Jerusalem, now down to Galilee, now sitting arguing with Nicodemus, now pouring out His heart to His disciples, now in calm dignity replying to the taunts of the Pharisees. His own conception of the law of life is clear enough. "My meat is to do the will of Him that sent Me," He once said. It was God's will, not His own choice, not their own fitness, not even directly the good of the men about Him, that made him do the acts and incur the contacts that filled up His days. God willed these things. That was the unity in which all His experiences found their consistency. That was the soil in which their roots were set, from which they drew their nourishment. That, in the deeper meaning, was His life; the Law by which He lived, the will of God.

And yet there is another step. A law is not the final life. It cannot be. Law is external, but life is something which must fill every inmost part of a man's being. It must think in his brain, throb in his heart, and make the will leap like a resolute muscle to its task. A law cannot do that. It is not intimate enough. That must be done by something which is part of the man himself, something that is his own, some form in which the world outside himself has passed into his being and given itself to him, some conception which is a fountain of force and inspiration. Now, all that can only be fulfilled in some controlling and inspiring idea, some idea or conception which, taking possession of the intelligence, has then set fire to the affections, and so possesses the whole man. When you get back to that you can go back no farther. Here, then, we are, where we have started in each of our lectures. Here we are, once again at the idea of Jesus. That idea, as I conceive it, as I am sure you know by this time that I conceive it, is the fatherhood of God to man, to be made known by Jesus to mankind through the clear manifestation of His own sonship to God. Ideas make for themselves laws by their own inherent and divine creativeness. The law which Christ's sonship to God makes is obedience to God. The way in which Christ's obedience to God enters into Him and becomes more than a rule of action, becomes the very element in which He lives, is by its being perpetually fastened to, perpetually fed out of, His idea that He was the Son of God. In that idea, that fundamental conception of His mind, that fundamental affection of His soul, you find at last what you have been seeking, His real life. You can go back no farther. You have laid your hand upon the Man of the Gospels, where His being becomes one with the uncaused Existence of eternity. At last you have found the true life of Jesus.

I think that it is like that marvel and mystery of nature, so familiar and yet so strange, so perpetually repeated in our sight and yet so far away from the apprehension of anything in us save our imagination, — the wonder that fills the woods and will burst forth between the very bricks of city streets, — the ever old, ever new mystery of the growing and flowering of a plant. The flower opens on the stalk; but the flower is not the life, for you may pluck it off leaf by leaf, and the plant still lives. The stalk builds its strong fibre; but its fibres are not life, for they may all be perfect and the plant be dead. The hungry roots reach out into the fertile ground; but the roots are not life, only wonderful channels to bear the life that has been given them. Not until you see the earth give itself to the plant, and, turning into sap, send itself through the waiting veins until it flushes into color far up in the air, — not until then have you gone back where you can go back no farther, and really found the life. So here is the perfect flower of the life of Jesus. It is the blood-red flower of the cross. Is that pain life? Surely not. The thief beside him bears pain too, and we can call it only death. Is life, then, the experience that brings the pain? The injustice of the rulers, the mocking of the people, the brutality of the soldiers, — is that His life? No, surely not. The deadest soul might have encountered all of these experiences. Is it, then, that deep compulsion that lay underneath it all? Is it that necessity which has been on Him all His days that He should do His Father's will, that compulsion which has brought Him to the cross? Not yet have we attained the life, for mere obedience may be mere death. But behind all there lies the idea of Jesus, that God is His Father, and that He may make these men know that He is their Father too. When that is touched, behold the miracle! See how the dry roots of obedience fill themselves with love; see how the hard stalk of experience grows soft and pliable with purpose; and then see how the flower of pain utters a life profoundly deeper than itself, and tells the world that story which it is the struggle of all pain and pleasure in the career of Christ to tell, which all healthy pain or pleasure in the career of man is tempting him to learn, — of man's unbroken sonship to his Father, of the belonging of his soul to the soul of God.

I have dwelt long upon this analysis of the real seat of influential life in Jesus, because only by understanding this can we truly understand the position and meaning which He would give to suffering and enjoyment in His life or in ours. I trust that the importance of what I have been saying will appear as I go on. It will be enough at present to suggest as the principle which governs all Christ's treatment of these phenomena of life that in His thought of them they are phenomena. They are not essential, they are accidental. Consequently they are neither to be sought nor shunned, but to be accepted as they come, with a welcome which goes below them and deals with the conditions out of which they spring. Jesus always thinks of Himself as undergoing the will of God, because God is His Father. The pain and pleasure which come to Him in undergoing that will come not simply with their own inherent qualities of comfort or discomfort, but with the values which they get from that obedience of which they are the signs and consequences. This is the key to all His attitude towards them. And of this principle all the special study to which we now proceed will be in illustration.

Our subject properly divides itself into two parts: 1. What is the position and meaning of enjoyment and sorrow in the life of Jesus? 2. What is the position and meaning of enjoyment and sorrow in the life of His disciples? It is once more a Biblical study in which we are to engage, and the ground over which we are to range is the rich field of the four Gospels.

I ask you to recall as simply as you can, as much as possible as if you read it for the first time, the story of the life of Jesus. One of the things which, if we can do that, will, I think, impress us most, will be the constant presence of the emotions of pleasure and of pain in the experience of Him whose history we are reading, whose person in those graphic pages stands before us. We shall have occasion in a few moments to go over in detail the series of special instances; but just now remember merely the general impression which the story makes. It is a country with an atmosphere. Clouds and sunshine are playing across its surface all the time. The actual features of the varied landscape are always changing their aspect with the light that falls upon them. The special events which happen have an additional character as they lie in the light or in the shade. What a landscape would be which had no atmosphere above it, which received no shadow and no sunlight on it, that would a life be which was made up of events but knew no emotions. A dreadful place! Hills, valleys, oceans, rivers, fields, all perfect, all grouped with one another in completest symmetry, but all bathed in one monotonous, unchanging light; all the same every day and every hour; no soft transitions from the solemn gloom into the happy brilliance, none of that change of smile and frown with one another that makes us feel the fitness when we talk about the "face of nature"! A dreadful world! A world in which no character could grow, no manhood ripen. The life of Jesus shows us no such world as that. It is changing every moment with the light and shade. A sensitiveness whose quickness to impressions we feel almost painfully trembles in every line. Only — and here is where the principles which I have just been stating show their influence in His life — Jesus, with all His sensitiveness to pain and joy, still never allows pain or joy to be either the purpose of life or the test of life with Him. The country, to renew our figure, is bright with sunshine or serious with shadow, and gets its ever-changing beauty from their constant alternation; but it never sets itself to work to make the clouds whose shadows are to rest upon it, nor does it judge its landscape by the special gloom or glory which is cast on it at any moment. So, to speak not in figure, the sensitiveness of Jesus to pain and joy never leads Him for a moment to try to be sad or happy with direct endeavor; nor is there any sign that He ever judges the real character of Himself or any other man by the sadness or the happiness that for the moment covers His life. He simply lives, and joy and sorrow issue from His living, and cast their brightness and their gloominess back upon His life; but there is no sorrow and no joy that He ever sought for itself, and He always kept a self-knowledge underneath the joy or sorrow, undisturbed by the moment's happiness or unhappiness. They were like ripples on the surface of the stream, made by its flow, and, we are ready to imagine, enjoyed by the stream that made them, not sought by the stream for themselves, nor ever obscuring the stream's consciousness of its deeper currents. The supreme sorrow of the cross was never sought because it was sorrowful, and even while He hung in agony it never obscured the certainty of His own holiness in the great Sufferer's soul. These are the perpetual characteristics of the emotional life of Jesus, which our theology has often conjured out of sight, but which are of unspeakable value, as I think; for a clear understanding of them puts the Man who suffered and enjoyed more than any other man that ever lived in a noble and true relation to His suffering and joy, and makes His pain and pleasure a gospel to men in their sadness and their gladness everywhere.

I turn to a more minute examination of the illustrations of this. The pleasures and sufferings of Jesus lie in three different classes, and each of them demands our careful study.

The first class is composed of those which belonged to His physical nature,—those which could not have come to Him, which could not come to any man, except through the medium of a human body. It is good to see how manifold these joys and sorrows are. They begin in that strange, half-conscious life of infancy, where it is always so hard to estimate pleasure and pain, where it is so hard to tell what value to give to a cry that issues from an infant's lips or a smile that plays across his face. And yet the pain and delight of childhood we know are realities, inextricably snarled in with the first possession of a mortal body which breathes the breath of this alert and exacting world. The poverty and privation of the inn at Bethlehem and the forced and hurried journey into Egypt are instances of what I mean. They are not events on which we need to dwell. What they were to Jesus we cannot tell. They touch the outmost rim of the capacity of pain; but they open the way, for what comes afterwards. They declare what life is going to mean to this new mortal who has come into its power. They are the first few notes, not clearly intelligible in themselves, but giving us the key in which the opening life is to be lived. But as soon as the dim thicket of infancy opens into the clear path of manly life it becomes apparent that all the spiritual experiences of Jesus have an almost unexampled association with His physical life. Very few men's souls are so bound in with their bodies as was His with the frame He wore. At the very outset of His public career, when His self-understanding was gathering itself up for the work He had to do, He went away into the desert and was tempted. What happened there is at once one of the most mysterious and one of the most intelligible passages in the life of Jesus. To any man who has been young, who has faced life, who has listened while many voices called him to turn aside into plausible paths, and the one great voice of the God of Duty called him right onward to whatever might await him, — to every such man the essential meaning of the Temptation is beyond all doubt. At the same time its special scenery and action is very vague. Material fact and impalpable vision shoot through each other and cannot be unsnarled. But this, at least, is plain, — the body shared in the experience. Long, painful hunger went before the spiritual trial, and it is out of lips at once weak and tense with physical exhaustion that the pattern answers of all tempted souls proceed. By and by came another event which brings something of the same confusion of the mysterious and the intelligible. Jesus goes up into another mountain, and is transfigured. Indeed, in many respects this story belongs beside the story of the Temptation. The two mountains are the complements of one another. As the Temptation was the typical utterance of the perplexed conditions of human living, so the Transfiguration was the irrepressible utterance of the essential glory of human nature filled with divinity, reclaimed and openly asserted to be the Son of God. And in the Transfiguration, as in the Temptation, the body has its share. Not merely does the soul enjoy sublime converse with God and with the past. A sweet and awful gladness shines out from the face and hands, and even pierces from the hidden limbs through the coarse garments which shine "white as the light." I do not know the meaning of it all, but I know that what came to the spiritual came in some echo to the physical, and the body shared the gladness of the soul. And when we turn the page again and look into Gethsemane, the same completeness of the human life is there. "Being in an agony, He prayed more earnestly, and His sweat was as it were great drops of blood." However it may be swathed about and purified and glorified by the suffering of the consecrated soul, there was physical pain there in the Garden on the night before the cross. The next day came the cross itself, and the struggle of the devoutest souls with themselves has always been to keep the sight of the body's agony from monopolizing all their pity, and hiding from their sight the nobler and deeper suffering of the tortured spirit of the Crucified. In all of these scenes, is it not striking to see how the body bore the spirit company, how there came no spiritual delight or misery but that the physical chords were struck and could be heard sounding through the finer and more subtle music?

Again, it is not possible for one who really wants to know the sort of life that Jesus lived to turn away indifferently from what the people said about Him who used to see Him every day. Morning by morning, night by night, He went about those strange old streets where men looked at Him curiously, — exactly as we should look at any wondrous life that came and set itself in the familiar framing of these streets which we know so well. All the more, often, because they had no keen spiritual sympathy with Him, the outward life which He lived photographed itself upon their watchful observation. They were like reporters, not like disciples, and so their superficial account of what He did was perhaps all the more true. What did they say? One day He told them what He had often overheard: "The Son of man is come eating and drinking, and ye say, Behold a gluttonous man and a wine-bibber." Coarse, brutal, full of hostile caricature, no doubt the words are; but still they give us the sort of picture which we would like to have, from his foe's pencil, of any man whom we desired to know. At least there must be an indication in what direction His life was lived. No man with callous, stolid body, that could not suffer and could not enjoy, could ever have been taunted with that peculiar tone of mockery.

But there is something else in Jesus that always gives me a profound and vivid sense of how that human body which He wore was full of the capacity of suffering, and of how large a part of His total experience its emotions made. The fear of death, or rather, perhaps, the fear of dying, is something almost wholly physical. I know it is not conscience, — it is not the dread of meeting, as we feebly say, a God with whom she has lived in tenderest and most trusting communion for these forty years, — I know it is not these that make a true, pure saint turn white-cheeked and tremble when you go and tell her that she is to die. The emotion really has its birth where you behold its symptoms, in the body. It is the flesh that shrinks from the thought of dissolution with as truly a physical instinct as that with which the finger draws back from the knife that pricks it. Now through the Gospels there runs, almost from the beginning, a Via Dolorosa whose stones you can almost feel still tremble under the feet of Jesus walking to His more and more clearly realized death. One day at Cæsarea Philippi we can begin to trace it first. "From that day forth began Jesus to shew unto His disciples how that He must suffer many things of the elders and chief priests and scribes, and be killed." Then down in Galilee, "Jesus said unto them, The Son of man shall be betrayed into the hands of men, and they shall kill Him." Then, on the way up to the city where the cross was waiting, "Behold we go up to Jerusalem, and the Son of man shall be betrayed, and they shall condemn Him to death, and shall deliver Him to the Gentiles to crucify Him." It is a horror that belongs to a man whose body loves to live. "If it be possible, let this cup pass from Me." It was the cup of death, long watched and waited for, at last felt pressing with its cold rim on the lips. "It is finished." It was the same cup, drained at last, and the body giving itself over to the peace of death which lay on the other side of the dreadfulness of dying.

It is an unnatural, a somehow unhumanized eye that does not find these signs of the physical sensibility of Jesus scattered all through the Gospels. A poor sick woman crawls up and lays her finger on His garment's hem. Instantly He turns and asks, "Who touched Me?" He has felt her finger through the sensitive body and the sensitive soul together. Who can picture the pain and pleasure which always must have been beating into His nature through the sensitive substance of a body such as that?

But there is another region in which the physical conditions are unmistakably active, while it yet lies close on the borders of the purely spiritual being. Into that region we must follow Jesus before we can understand all the susceptibility to pain and joy that was bound up with the body that He wore. It is the region in which man feels the influences of external nature, and gathers delight or sorrow, is exalted or depressed, by the touches of the world around him. How wide and rich that region is in the best and completest men, all of us know; and I do not believe that any one can consider the way in which Jesus treated the world of nature, and especially can read His parables, without being sure that He lived in that region and was open to its influences always. "Consider the lilies of the field, how they grow," He cried, as they walked together, treading the autumnal crocus under foot. "Lift up your eyes and look on the fields, for they are white already to harvest." So He caught the picture of His truth as He sat by the well at Sichem and gazed down the bright open valley that leads toward Jerusalem. "When it is evening ye say, Fair weather, for the sky is red; and in the morning, Foul weather to-day, for the sky is red and lowering." So the influence of the sky overhead flowed down into His teaching. And in one parable — so short, so perfect, the exquisite jewel among the parables — all the work that He was doing, all the promise of God for humanity, shone out in the picture which had sunk into His soul in countless quiet walks through peaceful fields. "So is the kingdom of God as if a man should cast seed into the ground, and should sleep and rise night and day, and the seed should spring up and grow he knoweth not how." In all these there is pleasure. Joy comes in through the quick, delighted eyes, and runs through all the physical frame, which is part of that natural beauty to which it responds, — a joy that interprets to the healthy man the happiness of the happy brutes, as there is another joy that gives him some understanding of the bliss of God.

"How good is man's life, the mere living; how fit to employ
All the heart and the soul and the senses forever in joy!"

This is the joy that sings itself under the deep lessons of the parables, like the music under the pathos of a hymn, or the tingle of blood under the solemn consecration of the soldier who rushes to the fight.

And now what is the meaning of this sensibility to pain and pleasure which belonged to His body? What did it mean to Jesus? It is not hard to read. It is a witness of the completeness of human life in Him. Pure health it is which answers instantly to external physical conditions with their appropriate reply. True healthiness is always sensitive. To go into any

Gethsemane and not to feel the body sympathize with the soul, is not completeness but meagreness of life. To stand where food is spread before us and either morosely to hate it or greedily to clutch it, both are morbid. Both the ascetic and the glutton are self-conscious. The true human being forgets the body, not because the body is detached and cast away, but because the body is doing its work perfectly, — as the passenger on the great ship forgets the engine only because the engine's healthy pulse has become part and parcel of his shipboard life.

And again, the physical sensibility of Jesus bore testimony to the condition of the world He dwelt in. How wonderfully interesting it becomes in this regard! The perfect health registers disorder by its pain as truly as it proclaims and praises order by its happiness. And here was Jesus, standing with His representative human body in this manifold and complicated world. How will the world utter itself on Him? Behold, now a quick pain leaps through Him as He treads on some serpent in the way; now a sweet joy falls through the body on the spirit, as the breath of heaven blows upon His cheek. Pain and joy, joy and pain, in quick succession! What shall we say? What can we say, but that here in the centre of the Bible the philosophy that runs through the Bible, the philosophy which makes man the centre and registering test of nature, comes to its perfection? The Old Testament had told of how nature to obedient man had been all good; how nature to man disobedient had declared its sympathy in thorns and thistles and angry beasts. The New Testament was to tell of a whole creation groaning and travailing, waiting for the redemption of the human body. Here in the midst of Scripture stands the sensitive body of the Son of Man, fully in the present lot of His brother men; and to Him the mottled world, the world that was God's child, and yet was full of selfishness and sin, the world whose name, as He Himself gave it, was the Prodigal Son,—a son, but prodigal; prodigal, yet a son,—to Him this mingled world declared itself in mingled pain and pleasure, and wrote the story of its own condition in what He suffered and enjoyed.

And yet once more. The physical sensitiveness of Jesus no doubt helped, as no other medium could have helped, that deep, mysterious process, the development of the self-consciousness of Jesus. Why should I not believe that out of the physical difficulties which tore His hands He plucked the full flower of His knowledge of His own soul, and, wrapped up at the heart of that, His knowledge of the soul of His Father? Why should I not believe that His gratitude for the pure joy of physical living was one of the doors through which He entered into the complete sense of how His soul's life issued from and belonged to God? That which is the sign of any condition always, by a subtle law, deepens and ripens and confirms that condition. And so when Jesus said to Pilate, who was threatening Him with the physical pain of crucifixion, "Thou couldst have no power at all against Me except it were given thee from above," it was not merely a testimony that He felt already the holding of His soul in His Father's everlasting hand, it was also a nestling of the soul yet more deeply and tenderly into the hollow of the hand that held it.

This was what the succession of physical pain and pleasure meant to Jesus. It was the witness of His complete human life; it was the register of the disordered world; and it was the instrument for the development of His spiritual consciousness. And now have we not the answer to our second question upon this first point? What did He intend that pain and joy should mean to His disciples? These same three things, no doubt. Think of the times when He distinctly recognized the susceptibilities of their bodily life. Once on the Sabbath day he walked through a cornfield, and the hungry men plucked the ripe ears and rubbed them in their hands and ate them. Jesus said, "The Son of man is Lord of the Sabbath." His recognition of human nature and its needs lay behind the positive institution which He did not dishonor. Even in Gethsemane the tired friends who were keeping Him company fell asleep; and it was only with the wonder of one who for the moment was out of the power or hope of rest that He dropped His gentle reproach upon them. When the crowd followed Him across the lake, He was as quick to see their starved faces as He was to read their sinful hearts. "I have compassion upon the multitude," He said, "because they continue with Me now three days and have nothing to eat." It is simply to Him the sign that they are men. He touches the fact of their humanity in helping them, and that seems to give Him joy. The same appeared when men came to Him and complained that His disciples were not ascetics like the disciples of John. "Why do the disciples of John fast often, but Thine eat and drink?" "Can ye make the children of the bridechamber fast while the bridegroom is with them?" He replied. That physical pleasure should be the accompaniment of spiritual joy, He accepted as part of the harmony of the universe.

Nor is it less true that Jesus accepted the pain of other men, like His own pain, as an utterance of the condition of the world in which they all were living together. When, as He put His fingers in the deaf man's ears and looked up to heaven before He gave the poor creature hearing, He sent a sigh up with the prayer, it must have been that He felt thr'ugh this one crack the whole tumult of the disturbed creation in which all deformity and suffering had their deep roots. And we may almost turn at random to His miracles: see Him with the nobleman who came from Capernaum to Cana, cultivating his faith at the same time that He cured his son; stand with Him in the boat and see Him send calm into the tempest and into His disciples' frightened hearts at once; look across the stormy water and see Him lift Peter out of the waves and out of his doubt at the same time, — to recognize how He always used the body's sensibilities to develop the soul's consciousness, how by physical pain and joy He helped the spirit to know itself and to know its Father.

To Jesus, and to His disciples, and to all men who know the bodily life as He knew it and taught them to know it, the pain and happiness of which the human body is capable must be very noble messages. When I suffer or when I enjoy, — when down these nerves the quick agony shoots and leaves me trembling like a poor tree which the blast has shivered, or when through the healthy blood peace runs like the sunlight on a flowing river, — when, in the aggregate of life, beneath affections, thoughts, dreams, memories, desires, there is always felt this human body with its pangs and blisses, what a noble meaning there is in it all as it lies open to the influence of Jesus! "Lo, I am human!" And all the dignity and pathos of humanity surrounds me. "Behold in what a disturbed and struggling world I live!" And hope and fear, — twin captains of the soul, — patience and expectation, spring to life. "See here, touching this very flesh of mine, the fingers of the hand whose heart is my Father's," and through the passions which the body feels opens a way into the deepest woes and loftiest pleasures, which can belong only to the sons of God.

I must pass on to the joys and sorrows of the next deeper grade, to those which have their roots not in the senses but in the affections. They are a great deal deeper. The way in which the body's pains will easily be borne or the body's pleasures easily be sacrificed in order that we may delight ourselves in the indulgence of the affections or escape their wounds, is proof enough how we all feel that the heart is the true seat of life, and not the body. "When the numbness comes up to my heart, then I shall depart," said Socrates, after he had drunk the poison. The passions of the body may mean much, but they can never mean life or death. Only in the loves we have for others than ourselves can we truly live or die.

When we come to study this region of the life of Jesus, the field that opens to us is very wide. We can do hardly more than just point out its features. And the most prominent among them all must be the absorbing affection of His life, the pure love that He had for His Father, God. We go about and about this centre of the life of Jesus, we talk of what it made Him do, we talk of how He tried to communicate it to those whom He taught. But it very often seems to me as if those of us who have read the Gospels most have but seldom grasped the love which Jesus had for His Father and understood it as a simple consciousness; not as a motive, but as a pure atmosphere of pleasure, the perpetual bright flower of the absolute unity of will which was between them. There are some simple expressions of this in the Gospel, which get their profoundest beauty only as we think of them with the most absolute simplicity. Jesus one evening went away by Himself into a mountain and "continued all night in prayer to God." We say that He was seeking preparation for the solemn task of selecting His disciples, which He undertook the next day. Certainly the communion of that night must have prepared Him for the task, but in itself what was it but the simple resting of one nature on the bosom of the nature which it loved, and in the fact of loving which it found its perfect joy? I think that if we go behind that simplicity we lose the beauty and majesty of it all. The most majestic is always the simple, not the complicated. And so it is not what I may picture to myself that Jesus asked of His Father in those sacred hours; it is simply that Jesus was with His Father, every interference of the daytime being completely set aside; that life touched life in the complete communion of love, — that is the final fact on which the mind which is seeking the happiness of Jesus in the life of the affections rests without asking for analysis.

That is only one instance. Another comes

before us in that deep and eager cry which broke forth from the lips of Jesus on the cross. "My God, My God," He cried out, "why hast Thou forsaken Me?" I do not pretend to understand all the meaning of that cry. Nobody understands it. What wonder is it if, when the last words of any faithful man finishing his noble life have always something in them which the most true and lifelong sympathy that stands about his bed cannot comprehend, the dying words of Jesus should have mystery in them and suggest strange questions which we cannot answer? But though I do not understand it fully, I know that I come nearest to its meaning when its meaning seems to me most simple. It is pure love, — love thwarted, hindered, and perplexed, but yet pure love, with that triumph which love always carries in its very existence whether it reach its object and call back response or not. Jesus does not beg for release. He does not even ask for vindication. He only utters love. And that cry after His Father lets us look down into His heart and see that in loving His Father and being loved by Him was His perpetual joy.

And yet see how this cry of Jesus illustrates what I said about the position which pleasure and pain always took in His life. They are always subordinated to the doing of a will, which will in its turn gets its value from the idea which inspires it. So here. The joy of loving and the pain which only love can bring beat tumultuously together in this cry. But underneath them both there is obedience, and the idea from which obedience proceeds. Not for one moment does He think of coming down from the cross to find His Father. Whether He find Him or lose Him, whether the issue of His love be the perfect joy of union or the exquisite suffering that separation brings, He must obey Him first. Even if His doing of His Father's will seems to shut Him out of His Father's presence, there cannot be a question; the will must be done. Oh, how often souls have forgotten, as they weighed the raptures, the ecstasies of faith against its hard and present duties when the two seemed to be not compatible with one another,— how often they have forgotten that the question which was greater and more sacred of the two, the rapture or the obedience, was settled once forever on the cross!

We pass from this supreme affection of Jesus to the others which are included in it. I had occasion in my last lecture to speak of the relations which Jesus held to those persons who were immediately connected with Him by the ties of kindred. I refer again to the family life in which He lived, only to notice what was the kind of pleasure and suffering that it brought to Him which He could not otherwise have met. That it did bring Him both there can be no doubt. In all his intercourse with John the Baptist we never can lose remembrance of the relationship between them. The old pictures which have grouped them as children by the Virgin's knee express a feeling which we can never cast aside. It is impossible to make their connection simply official. When John baptizes Jesus, it is a kinsman's hand that leads the exalted youth into the water. And by and by, when the disciples went to the prison and took the body of the murdered Baptist and buried it, and came and told their Master, it was for one of His own family blood as well as for one of His own divine spirit that Jesus mourned. And there is another passage which always seems to me to open a glimpse of the family affection which was in the heart of Jesus. He had avoided Judea because it was not safe for Him to work there. He was laboring in Galilee. And his brethren came to Him and said, "Depart hence and go into Judea. If Thou do these things, show Thyself unto the world." It was almost a jeering mockery. "Neither did His brethren believe in Him," the writer adds. The pain of having those doubt Him who ought to know Him best, of having His own flesh and blood turn on Him and mock Him, — it is evident that Jesus knew what that pain was, and that it was something peculiar to Him, something different from the unbelief and hostility of the promiscuous crowd. Then turn for another instance to the crucifixion, to those few hours of distress which sometimes seem to epitomize all that there was in His entire life. "There stood by the cross of Jesus His mother and His mother's sister," and just as He was dying the Sufferer turned and gave His mother to the care of His disciple. " Woman, behold thy son!" "Son, behold thy mother!" It was a pang within all the other pangs, a woe that perceptibly added to their wretchedness, when among the faces that pitied Him He saw her face who bore Him, the face into which He had looked up from His cradle. When I think over these three stories, it seems to me that I discover what the real meaning was of that additional element of joy and pain which came to Jesus through His family affections. In each I seem to see that the family relationship was representative of something deeper that lay in behind. His special connection with those special lives was, as it were, the manifestation point of His relationship to all the world. What He was to those brethren who had always lived in the same house with Him he was essentially to all mankind. In them He realized with peculiar vividness what was true of all the world. All men were sons of God along with Him, but that sonship shone forth in a peculiar clearness in these men, who were also of Mary's blood as well as He. It gave him joy when any of His brethren in the most remote degree realized the sonship which was revealed in Him or (as He himself expressed it) came to the Father through Him. But that joy was vividest when one of His brethren in the nearest and most special sense attained that high belief. The pain of any human being touched Him, but in His mother's pain humanity pressed itself closest to His sensibility and gave Him a special distress proportioned to His special love. In general, the woes and pleasures through His family affections were those which belonged to His whole contact with humanity, only deepened and emphasized and vivified by the particular dearness in which these kindred lives stood to His own.

And yet I hasten on to say that such an account of the emotions which belong to Christ's domestic life does not in the least conflict with that spontaneous character which is of the every essence of such emotions always. Indeed, the best and noblest natures, as I think, are marked by hardly anything so much as this, — the simultaneous spontaneousness and reasonableness of the lives they live. One kind of man is all spontaneous, and can furnish no account of what he feels and does. Another kind of man is all reasonable, and lets no impulsive action slip from his will till it has accounted for itself to his conscious understanding. Both of these men are partial. There is a man who is more complete than either, who is as impulsive as a child and yet in the heart of whose impulsive action there always lies the true reasonableness of manhood. He does the natural human acts because he must do them, and yet he knows why he does them. The spontaneousness does not obscure the reason, and the reason does not hamper and clog the spontaneousness. So it always seems to me that it is with Jesus. He presses His brother's hand with brotherly affection. His brother's sneer wounds Him as no stranger's can. His mother's sorrow enters into its own secret chamber of sympathy in Him where no other sorrow can intrude. And yet all the while, with all the instinctive value which He gave to them for their own sake, these home affections all are ties to bind Him to humanity, windows through which He looks into the depths of human life, interpretations to His soul of the wider brotherhood in the vaster family.

Surely there is here a noble indication of what the family affections as sources of suffering and happiness may be to all men, of what they must be to all men who dwell in them within the larger family which Jesus shows. It is dreadful if we lose their spontaneousness. Beyond all analysis there lies the relation which every true son holds to a true father. It is a final fact. You cannot dissolve it in any abstract theory. It issues from the mysterious sympathy of the two lives, one of which gave birth to the other. It has ripened and mellowed through all the rich intercourse of dependent childhood and imitative youth and sympathetic manhood. It is an eternal fact. Death cannot destroy it. The grown-up man feels his father's life beating from beyond the grave, and is sure that in his own eternity the child relation to that life will be in some mysterious and perfect way resumed and glorified, that he will be something to that dear life and it to him forever. All this remains Its bright spontaneousness nothing is allowed to tarnish. And yet the adult son delights to learn how, through his intimacy with that nature out of which his sprang, he is introduced into an understanding of the whole human race. In a deeper sense than we are apt to give the words, his father "brings him into the world." His father's life is to him the illumination point of all humanity. In loving his father he loves his race. And all the joy and pain, all the richness and pathos of his home life, while they keep their freshness and peculiar sanctity, have in them and below them all the multitudinous happiness and sorrow of the larger life in the great household of the world. The child feels something of this truth by instinct. The thoughtful man delights to realize it more and more as he grows older.

To come back, however, to the life of Jesus, we are aware that His relations to those who held the ties of kinship with Him, while they were clear and real, were not a large or promi nent element in His life. He quickly went beyond the household of the carpenter in His eagerness to attain the household of God. He was the brother of all men. And the truth of all the emotion which filled the social life of Jesus when we sum it up, seems to be this: that all multiplied and deepened relationships with men bring mingled joy and sorrow; a joy and a sorrow which it is not possible to separate and weigh against each other, because they are so subtly and intricately mingled that the joy makes part of the sorrow and the sorrow makes part of the joy, and you cannot take away either without finding that the other has eluded you; a joy and sorrow also which no man can ever gain by directly and deliberately seeking them, but which come unsought to every man who, regardless of the pleasure or the pain they bring, enters into profound connections with his fellow-men. These are the two key truths of any social life which goes beyond a club acquaintance or a parlor friendship. He will certainly fail who hopes to know men deeply and only to get happiness — never to get anxiety, distress, disappointment —

out of knowing them; and he has mistaken the first idea of human companionship who seeks friendships and contacts with mankind directly and simply for the pleasures they will give him.

Now Jesus quietly and steadily met both these laws. He calmly deepened His relations to mankind as much as possible, accepting all the pain that such profound relationships might bring; and always with Him the happiness or unhappiness of His associations were but accidents, and not the final purposes for which He won His friends or encountered the hostility of His enemies. Here is one of His disciples, Simon Peter. Two picturesque moments stand out in the history of the intercourse of Jesus with that interesting man. At the foot of Hermon, tempted by a question of his Master, Peter burst forth with a hearty and enthusiastic utterance of his conviction of the divine nature which had been steadily impressing itself upon him. "And Jesus answered and said unto him, Blessed art thou, Simon Barjona, for flesh and blood hath not revealed it unto thee, but My Father which is in heaven." In the high-priest's house at Jerusalem, when Jesus was standing a culprit on the night of His arrest, waiting for the scourging and the cross, He overheard this same Peter say twice, "I do not know Him," when some servants questioned him about the prisoner whose fate was the question of the hour. "And the Lord turned and looked on Peter. And Peter went out and wept bitterly." See what two influences came out of this friendship. See what joy and sorrow issued from the bosom of this love. See how the joy at hearing the confession of such a profound, far-reaching truth as His own divinity must have been full of fear which was almost certainty that the disciple would fail in some of the inevitable applications of the truth which he must be so imperfectly appreciating even while he enthusiastically proclaimed it. See how the suffering which the treason brought must still have had in it a consolation, as Jesus detected in the very passion of the denial the crushed remonstrance of the love which, even under the denial, was living still. Or take a yet harder case. Jesus had another disciple whom He saw slipping more and more away from Him, who He saw would some day betray Him with the worst ingratitude. And yet I think that every man whose sad and anxious office it has ever been to try to lift a soul which in spite of all his struggles has been always sinking deeper and deeper into the depths, will bear me witness that in the patience and wisdom and faithfulness which his Master lavished upon Judas Iscariot for years there must have been a pathetic pleasure, peculiar and subtle because of the growing hopelessness of results which compelled each effort to find its satisfaction in its own essential nature. It must have had something of the delight in mere service with which one watches at the bedside of a sick friend, of whose recovery all hope is gone. And both in Peter and in Judas the second of the truths of which I spoke appears,— that it was not for the joy or for the sorrow that their society would bring that Jesus sought them. Peter and Judas alike He sought because they were the sons of God; the pain or pleasure they would give Him came afterwards and as an accident.

Ir all of Christ's associations the same inevitable mingling of the sad and glad appears. There was a little family at Bethany in which He often made His home, and the last time He left the hospitable door He carried out with Him two memories, — the memory of how the eyes of Mary had looked up into His face, eager with the desire to understand all His sacred truth, and the memory of how the same eyes had streamed with tears beside her brother's tomb. The same voices of the populace at Jerusalem which cried "Hosanna!" cried "Crucify him!" before the week was done. The happiness of promising heaven to a dying thief was filled with pity that only by a torturing death had the poor wretch been brought into the sight and hope of life. One day He saw a poor widow in the Temple give a true charity; but the same sensitiveness of soul which made Him find pleasure in her simple act laid Him open to the distress which only such a soul could feel at the ostentatious hypocrisy of the Pharisees. And all through His life the deep, enthusiastic happiness at giving men the chance of their divine inheritance was mingled with the distress of knowing that men who would not take what He held out to them must be worse off than if He had not come to them. "He that heareth My word hath everlasting life," and "On whomsoever this stone shall fall it shall grind him to powder," — the opposite fates of men, with the emotions they awakened, — the two were always on His heart together and crowded each other on His lips.

So it must always be. To be a true minister to men is always to accept new happiness and new distress, both of them forever deepening and entering into closer and more inseparable union with each other the more profound and spiritual the ministry becomes. The man who gives himself to other men can never be a wholly sad man; but no more can he be a man of unclouded gladness. To him shall come with every deeper consecration a before untasted joy, but in the same cup shall be mixed a sorrow that it was beyond his power to feel before. They who long to sit with Jesus on His throne may sit there if the Father sees them pure and worthy, but they must be baptized with the baptism that He is baptized with

All truly consecrated men learn little by little that what they are consecrated to is not joy or sorrow, but a divine idea and a profound obedience, which can find their full outward expression not in joy, and not in sorrow, but in the mysterious and inseparable mingling of the two.

There yet remains one other class of pleasures and sufferings which belong to all devoted and ideal natures, and in which Jesus had a share. It consists of the moral joys and pains, of those which come from the acute perception of right and wrong, of moral fitness or unfitness in the things about us. You cannot put a man very high unless you give him a good share of that quality. Merely to see that things are right or wrong, and not to feel a pleasure in their rightness and a pain in their wrongness, does not indicate a finely moulded character. The moral perceptions, even the moral obediences, do not make a full moral life. The moral emotions must be there too. That such a power as this was in Jesus nobody can doubt who knows Him. And yet we are a good deal surprised, I think, when we survey His history and see how few are the moments in which this power prominently appears. The reason is that the life of Jesus, and all His thoughts and feelings, had personal shapes and directions. We do not know how largely this is true until we read the Gospels with this thought in our minds. The great moral enthusiasts kindle when they see a good deed done, rejoice in the progress of humanity, have a keen happiness when some new instance brings out the fitness for virtue which is in the whole great world, and on the other hand suffer as if a spear pierced them or a club smote them when a bad action makes a discord and wrongs the fundamental purpose of the world. There is very little indeed of that in Jesus. We cannot think of Him as a pure moral enthusiast. With Him almost everything is personal. He is glad when a man is good because the man's own life is illuminated, and still more because the man glorifies His Father which is in heaven. A wickedness wounds Him because it is a degradation to the man who does it and an insult to God. Behold Him as He goes into the Temple, which the greedy people had turned into a market-house. It is "My Father's house" for which he is so jealous. It is no abstraction of reverence for which He burns. It is exactly as if a child came home and found his mother's chamber turned into a huckster's shop. It is as literal, as personal, as that. The profound sense of unfitness, of discord, is there, but it is held in solution in this more vehement feeling of personal wrong. It is this personalness of all His moral enthusiasms, as it seems to me, that keeps us from ever feeling or fearing in Jesus any of that moral pedantry — or what, with a word that has no dignified equivalent, we call that priggishness — which haunts the words of the moral enthusiasts who kindle at the harmonies and discords of abstractions, whether they talk as utilitarians or as transcendentalists.

Nevertheless, though this is true, the sense of the absolute must underlie and must appear through the personal enthusiasms of Jesus. Otherwise the moral quality would evaporate, and His personal emotions would come to be only mere fondnesses and prejudices. And there are instances enough in which we can feel, beating and shining through His personal affections, the delight and sorrow with which His soul recognized the essential qualities of holiness and sin. I have already spoken of the indignation which possessed Him in the desecrated Temple. As an illustration of the opposite emotion, there occurs that beautiful outburst in which, almost with surprise, certainly with a sudden overflow of gladness, as He saw the perfection of the method of God's treatment of the world and revelation of Himself through innocence, Jesus breaks out and cries, "I thank Thee, O Father, Lord of heaven and earth, that Thou hast hid these things from the wise and prudent and hast revealed them unto babes." What a happy heart is there! It is all personal, and yet the personalness holds clearly in its heart a sense of the beauty of a moral idea,—the idea that the profoundest belongs to the purest, the loftiest truth to the innocent and guileless heart. One day a centurion came to Jesus and wanted Him to work a miracle; and as they talked about it, the simplicity of the man's trust came out. He illustrated His belief in the power of Jesus by describing his own relation to the forces which were under him. "I say to this man, Go, and he goeth ; and to another, Come, and he cometh." Instantly, as it would seem, so large and true a conception of the world all held together in one sublime system of authority and obedience, running up to the highest, running down to the least of its activities, filled the soul of Jesus with delight. "I have not seen so great faith, no, not in Israel," He said. One other day, in a remote country village, He met ten lepers. As the poor wretches stood afar off and cried to Him, He bade them go and show themselves to the priests. And as they went, lo, their leprosy was gone and they were clean. Then one of them turned back, all radiant with gratitude, and fell down at his healer's feet. National prejudice, — for the man was a Samaritan, — old bitterness, the selfishness which comes with sudden happiness, all these were broken through, and there he lay, all overwhelmed with thankfulness and love. Meanwhile the other nine went cheerily upon their way, meanly satisfied with the mere fact of health. There comes a sorrow and a joy into the face and words of Jesus which are primarily and formally personal, but are not wholly so. In at the heart of it, it is the joy which every noble heart feels at the very sight of gratefulness, and the pain that each true soul experiences at the very presence of ingratitude. That such things are, — their very being and essential qualities, — these are what wake responses of gladness or of sadness in the soul. You have to reach in and find that feeling underneath the personal emotions of Jesus. But it is always there. When He pities Jerusalem, His pity has an eternal dignity about it, because the woe which He commiserates is but part of the universal tragedy of sin. When the poor woman stops Him by the roadside, and with the wit of wretchedness claims even for a dog some crumb of the precious mercy, His praise of her is more than recognition of her quick rejoinder; it is a pleasure in the sight of that clear hold on the right of the weaker over the stronger which is part of the moral structure of the universe. And at the last, when the supreme joy of His life comes, and with an appeal to His Father's perfect knowledge He exclaims, "I have glorified Thee on the earth, I have finished the work that Thou gavest Me to do," there is heard inside of that appeal a pure joy in the establishment of righteousness and the setting up of the kingdom of salvation which is the basis of the personal gratulation that the words express. I must not multiply illustrations. I do not know one instance of Christ's joy in moral harmony that is not held in the bosom of some personal affection. But, on the other hand, I do not know one instance of personal affection which does not get its value from some moral emotion at the centre of it. That is the kind of moral enthusiasm which the influence of Jesus has spread throughout the world. It is not calm, cool approbation of goodness, it is delight in a good man, with which the Christian kindles. But it is always certainly his goodness in him — not his mere person, but the moral nature which his person vividly exhibits — that excites the Christian's admiration. And so it is neither an enthusiasm for goodness nor an enthusiasm of humanity that the influence of Jesus is creating in the world, but a communion of saints, — a race of men each delighting in the other for his holiness, and each delighting in holiness for the brightness that it gives the others' lives.

I do not think that it would be right to close this study of the pleasure and the pain which Jesus experienced and into which His disciples are constantly led, without saying two or three words upon a point which may often suggest a difficulty. I have been speaking of the certain satisfaction of His soul in moral fitness, in the harmony of righteousness. But, some one asks, how is it with those other harmonies in which we are always finding delight, the fitnesses which the æsthetic nature recognizes and loves? Was there anything of those in Jesus? Had He anything of what we call the sense of artistic beauty? Did He get any of that joy of taste of which our modern life makes so much? It is not an easy question to answer in a word. We may point to the special earnest purpose which filled all of the life of Jesus. We may say that

He who was walking on to Calvary had no time in the intenseness of His moral life for art and its luxuriousness. We may say that He was a Jew, and it was not in the nature of His race to gather from beautiful things that happiness which they imparted to the quick-eyed Greek. We may say that it was a mere question of the accidental circumstances and furniture of the life of Christ, that the physical sensibility and the moral impressibleness which we have been studying in Him make undoubtedly a large part, while undoubtedly they do not make the whole of that only half-accountable element in us which we call the æsthetic nature, and so that the capacity of the pleasure which that nature values only waited in Him for some circumstances to develop it. We may say that though Jesus made nothing of artistic beauty, yet His religion has made much of it, and out of Christianity the highest artistic life has come. We may say all these things, and no doubt all of them have truth. But still the great impression of the life of Jesus, as it seems to me, must always be of the subordinate importance of those things in which only the æsthetic nature finds its pleasure. There is no condemnation of them in that wise, deep life. But the fact always must remain that the wisest, deepest life that was ever lived left them on one side, was satisfied without them. And His religion, while it has developed and delighted in their culture, has always kept two strong habits with reference to art which showed that in it was still the spirit of its Master. It has always been restless under the sway of any art that did not breathe with spiritual and moral purpose. Never has Christian art reached the pure æstheticism of the classics. And in its more earnest moods, in its reformations, in its puritanisms, it has always stood ready to sacrifice the choicest works of artistic beauty for the restoration or preservation of the simple majesty of righteousness, the purity of truth, or the glory of God.

I have intimated already, once or twice to-day, what significance there is, not merely in the separate presences of joy and trouble in the life of Jesus, but also in the proportions which they hold to one another, and the way in which they are perpetually mingled. Let me recur to that a moment as I close. In that respect, as in many others, the last day of Jesus, the day of His crucifixion, presents no unreal picture of what His whole life was. That day, in spite of the tragedy which was ripening fast all through the morning, and the cross upon which the sun went down, was not all dark. Strange glimpses of a light which must have brought deep delight to the soul of Jesus shone out through all its course. Follow Him in your thought from the time when He met His disciples in Jerusalem the night before. First came the sitting down at supper with them, a feast of joy, the only familiar board at which we ever see Jesus through His life before His crucifixion. No sooner is He there, and the quiet happiness begun, than the disciples begin to quarrel about some foolish question of precedence, and Jesus is distressed. Then comes the beautiful action in which, as it were, He refreshes the joy of devotion which had filled the years of labor that were all over now.

He bends and washes the disciples' feet. No sooner is that done than Judas has to be convicted and dismissed. Then comes the bright moment when St. Peter bursts out with his promise of loyalty, followed the next instant by the Savior's sad prophecy of how near His disciple's weakness lay to his promised strength. Next follows the encouraging description of the Spirit of comfort and strength which was to come when Jesus had departed. Then, looking in the blank, unsuspicious faces of the men about Him, the Lord's voice sinks again as He foretells how they will be persecuted. In an instant all that is forgotten, and He is wrapt away from all the present in a celestial memory and a divine anticipation. "Now, O Father, glorify Thou Me with the glory which I had with Thee before the foundation of the world." With that ecstasy still filling Him, He goes out to the Garden and its agony. He is betrayed and deserted. Yet still one last poor flash of Peter's loyalty lightens the darkness for an instant. The denial, the trial, the scourging, the crucifixion, follow fast. Yet even in the midst of their horror there is room for some momentary gleams of joy. The wavering of Pilate; the cries of a few sympathetic voices among the hooting mobs as He passed through the street; the group of friends at the foot of the cross; and then that great joy which must have fallen into His spirit when from the other cross there came a cry of faith and hope; at last the utter satisfaction which fills His soul as He exclaims, "It is finished,"—all of these come in to show that the very agony of agonies was charged with the divine capacity of joy. As we gather the total impression of that wondrous day, how complete it is! How joy and sorrow interfuse and blend with one another! And the result is a new compound of life which is different from either. How evident it is that by some principle more deep than just that joy is pleasant and pain is hard to bear, they are distributed. It is as if Jesus walked under a cloud, and yet felt always that in the very substance of cloud there was suffused and softened light. The cloud had light in its darkness and darkness in its light; and so the explanation of it all was clear. A sunlight through the cloud

He felt, and behind the sunlight there must be a sun. Behind the bitter circumstances lay a law, the blessed law of obedience, which was fellowship with God ; and behind the law a truth which was God Himself.

Under that same cloud of circumstances we must walk; but if there is behind it, for us, too, that law and that truth which really made the life of Jesus, — the law of obedience and the truth of sonship, — then for us, too, light shall come through the cloud, and, mingling with its darkness, make that new condition in which it is best for a man's soul to live, that sweet and strong condition in which both joy and sorrow may have place, but which is greater than either of them, — the condition which He called peace.

IV.

THE INFLUENCE OF JESUS
ON THE INTELLECTUAL LIFE OF MAN

THE INFLUENCE OF JESUS

ON THE INTELLECTUAL LIFE OF MAN.

MEN and books have their favorite words. As the result of years of thoughtful life, of constant and studious dwelling upon one class of ideas, almost all men appropriate out of the great treasury of the language certain words which they make their own. Their friends grow used to hearing those words from their lips. The words become filled with their personality. Some color or shade or tone comes into them, as such a speaker habitually uses them, which indicates on which side he has approached their meaning, and they who honor him can hardly hear the words or speak them without entering into communion with his spirit.

If such an habitual use of certain words with certain tones is true and always fresh, if it does not come out of affectation and does not degenerate into mannerism, it often gives us the material for an excellent study of a man's life and nature. If he is only real, we may judge him by his words. As he speaketh with his mouth so is he. Tell me what words a man uses most, and reproduce for me the tones in which he speaks them, and I ought to be able to tell you a good deal about what sort of man he is. Count for me the favorite words of any book, and give me some idea of the association in which they stand, and I ought to know much of the book's quality and of what influence it will exert on those who read it.

I am to speak to-day of the influence of Jesus upon intellectual life, upon the world of thought; and I know no better way to approach a subject so interesting, so rich, and yet, as it seems to me, in its central point so simple, than by observing the prominence of one word and the very marked and characteristic way in which that word is used in the book which tells us most of what we know about the mind of Jesus. The book is the Gospel of St. John. The word is *truth*. It is only in that one book that the word is found upon the lips of Jesus with any of that special intonation which is peculiarly His own. There are three other Gospels, three other accounts of the Lord's life, but in neither of them does this, which is his most characteristic utterance in the fourth Gospel, once appear. I need not pause to say that such a fact suggests no real difficulty or discrepancy between the records. As different as Matthew and John were from each other, so different must have been the words of their Master which were caught in the memory and treasured in the heart of each. In the same way in which Zenophon and Plato both wrote of Socrates, and, holding different mirrors on different sides of that wonderfully interesting figure, have given us, not two Socrateses, but a completer Socrates than we could have had if only one of them had seen him and described him, so the first Gospel and the fourth enlarge each other, and the historic Jesus comes in the stereoscopic fulness of His recorded life and nature from the two. But Plato is more to us than Zenophon. The great Athenian lives in the Dialogues as he does not in the Memorabilia. And John is more to us than Matthew.

A word of Jesus constantly appearing in those discourses of Jesus which most impressed the most sympathetic and spiritual of his disciples will, if we can see what He meant by it, admit us very deeply into His heart and will. Such a word is *truth*, as it is used by Jesus constantly in the Gospel of St. John.

The word, then, is distinctly a word of the intellect. Whatever other elements may enter in, however it may enlarge itself and become a word of the entire nature, the intellectual element can never be cast out of it. He whose favorite word is truth must be a man who values intellectual life, who is not satisfied unless his own intellect is living, and who conceives of his fellow-men as beings in whom the intellect is an important and valuable part. This must belong to any habitual use of the word at all; and so, when we find it appearing constantly upon the lips of Jesus, in the record of that one of His disciples who understood Him best, we feel that we know this at least about Him, — that He cared for the intellect of man, that He desired to exercise some influence upon it, that He was not satisfied simply to win man's affection by His kindness, nor to govern man's will by His authority, but that He also wished to persuade man's mind with truth.

But we must know something more of what a man's conception about truth is before we can see what sort of influence he will exert upon men's intellects. Take Martin Luther's idea of truth, and Professor Huxley's idea, and Mr. Emerson's idea. How evident it is that the same word would be spoken indistinguishably different tones, and would strike with different force upon the hearer's ears and character as it came from three such different men. And so it is not enough that we should know the fact that Jesus constantly talked of truth. That would assure us that He sought an intellectual influence. We must also know what He meant by truth, and how He spoke of it. That will reveal to us what kind of intellectual influence it was that He desired. Let us turn then to some of the sayings of Jesus concerning truth. And, as we look at them, remember it is not the essential importance of what He says that we want to dwell on, but merely the indication in His saying of what He means by truth, of which He speaks so much. On one occasion, when He had been speaking very powerfully about His own personal relation to His Father, a great many of His hearers were persuaded and believed on Him. Then Jesus said to those Jews that believed on Him, "If ye continue in My word, then are ye My disciples indeed; and ye shall know the truth, and the truth shall make you free." That puzzled them. It stirred their Jewish blood. They told Him that they were born of Abraham, and were no man's slaves. "How sayest Thou, Ye shall be made free?" And Jesus answered them, "Truly I say unto you, every man that committeth sin is the servant of sin." That was the freedom that His truth was to bring, — a spiritual freedom, a freedom from wickedness, an untwisting of the tight cords from their hold on the personal nature. Truth was something which, when it came, would set the whole man free. By and by, in the same talk, He warmed into earnest pity not unmixed with indignation. Poor people! there they stood before Him, and would not, could not, understand the things He said to them. Would not and could not were all mixed together. But His indignation reaches back behind them. It cannot stop short of the Evil Spirit who is their deluder. "Ye are of your father the Devil, and the lusts of your father ye will do. He was a liar from the beginning and abode not in the truth." Again, see what a moral thing the truth is. He who does not abide in it is not merely a doubter, not merely a disbeliever, he is a liar. The truth is truthfulness. The subjective and objective lose themselves in one another. Then let the whole strain change. The warm discussion, the earnest indignation, is long past and over. Jesus is sitting with the men who loved Him in the quiet atmosphere of the Last Supper. A question of one of the disciples drew from Him the words which perhaps have fascinated and mysteriously fed as many souls as any words He ever spoke. "I am the Way, and the Truth, and the Life," He said. "I am the Truth." We must have some notion of what truth meant to Him which shall be large enough to contain those words. A truth which a man could be; a truth which could sum up and consist of personal qualities. Evidently it is not mere fact, this truth of His; not something merely done, merely made, and standing finished and recognizable, to be walked around and measured and studied on the outside by any patient eye. It is something living, something ever taking shape, something spiritual, and to be known only from the inside by spiritual sympathy. The evening passed on, and by and by Jesus began to unfold to His disciples the promise of what He would do for them even after He had left them. He is going to send them the Comforter, He says. And this Comforter, when He is come, is to "reprove the world of sin, of righteousness, and of judgment." Deep words, and full of meaning, much of which we have not fathomed yet. But this, at least, we know is in them. It is a spiritual helper who is coming; a soul coming to help souls; a moral master who shall judge and rule the moral life. And so when in a minute Jesus, as He goes on speaking, gives this Comforter another name, and says,

"When He, the Spirit of Truth, is come, He will lead you into all truth," we know again that truth cannot mean in Him merely objective verity; it must have in it the elements of character, since the leading of man into it by the Divine soul is to be the perfection of man's life. The evening wears on still, and by and by Jesus has ceased to speak directly to His friends. His voice is heard in prayer. And in His prayer there comes what we may almost call His summing up and report of all His life to His Father. "For their sakes I sanctify Myself, that they also might be sanctified through the truth," He says. It is His own character through which alone truth can come to make character in His disciples. It is the deep and satisfied declaration that His whole life had been given to seeking the fulfilment of the petition which He had just offered, "Sanctify them through Thy truth." The same crowded night slowly creeps away, and in the morning everything is once more altered. Jesus is standing before Pilate. And as the strange interview goes on, He has once more occasion to declare the sum and purpose of His life. "To this end was I born," He says, "and for this cause came I into the world, that I should bear witness to the truth. Every one that is of the truth heareth My voice." "Every man of the truth." Again you see how the air grows hazy with the meeting of the subjective and objective conceptions. They are words of character. A "man of the truth" is something more than a man who knows the truth, whose intellect has seized it; that, we are sure, would be the very tamest paraphrase of the suggestive words. It would take the whole life and depth out of them. A "man of the truth" is a man into all whose life the truth has been pressed till he is full of it, till he has been given to it, and it has been given to him, he being always the complete being whose unity is in that total of moral, intellectual, and spiritual life which makes what we call character. He is the man of whom Pilate's prisoner said, "He hears my voice." No wonder that Pilate, hearing a new sound in an old familiar word, felt all his old questions stir again within him, and asked with an interest which was too weary to be called a hope, "What is truth?"

These passages will show how the word truth sounds when Jesus says it. I have not hesitated to multiply them, because out of them all comes forth, I think, a perfectly clear conception of what the intellectual life was in Jesus. The great fact concerning it is this, that in Him the intellect never works alone. You never can separate its workings from the complete operation of the whole nature. He never simply knows, but always loves and resolves at the same time. Truth which the mind discovers becomes immediately the possession of the affections and the will. It cannot remain in the condition of mere knowledge. Indeed, knowledge is no word of Jesus. Solomon in the Book of Proverbs is always talking about knowledge. Jesus, in the Gospel of John, is always talking about truth. So genuine is the unity of His being, that what comes to Him as knowledge is pressed and gathered into every part of Him, and fills His entire nature as truth. The rays of intellectual light are absorbed into the whole substance of the spontaneous affections and the unerring will. The rig t and the true, the wrong and the false, are not separable from one another. The life is simple because of its completeness. It is the true unity of a man.

When we see how constantly it is the crudity of an unappropriated, unassimilated intellectuality that disappoints us in intellectual people; when we find ourselves turning away from many a learned man whose knowledge has not been pressed into character; when we find that the action of the intellect forcing itself upon our notice because it is working out of proportion to or out of harmony with the other parts of a man's nature, his conscience, his affections, and his active powers, always dissatisfies and makes us restless, and, with all the interest which we may feel in him, does not let us think that we have found the fullest and most perfect man,—when we see all this, it becomes clear to us what a distinguishing thing in Jesus was this unity of life in which the special action of the intellect was lost. We catch something of the spirit with which His disciple, fondly recurring years afterwards to the bright days when He first knew Jesus, twice used the same description of Him:

"The word was made flesh and dwelt among us, full of grace and truth." "The law was given by Moses, but by Jesus Christ came grace and truth."

We have only to dwell upon men's best conception of a Deity to see how distinct and how lofty this conception of intellectuality is which the life of Jesus sets before us. The partialness which we see in man, and which lets us easily divide our fellow-men into classes and label them the men of intellect or the men of action, passes away as we mount to any thought of God which is at all worthy of Him. What God knows is one and the same with the love with which He loves and the resolve with which He wills. You cannot draw a fence through the great ocean of infinity. Mythology dreams of its many gods with many functions. The moment that one God stands forth above all gods, the many things which the partial deities do lose themselves in the one perfect thing which the one only Deity is. And all wisdom unites with all power and all love no less in the guiding of a little child along the slippery path which leads to manhood, than in the vast conduct of the destinies of the colossal man who lives through all the generations of the race.

We need only to think of the kind of human creature who has always most easily commanded the instinctive admiration of his brethren, and we shall see that the same character reappears in him. It is not the intellectual man as such, not the man in whom intellect stands crudely forth as the controlling element in life, that other men are drawn to most. The greatest men that ever lived are those in whom you cannot separate the mental and moral lives. You cannot say just what part of their power and success is due to a good heart and what to a sound understanding. And in every circle there are apt to appear some persons of great influence and great attractiveness, of whom you never think as being specially intellectual. If any one calls them intellectual, it startles you; but as you think about your wonder, you discover that it does not come from an absence of the intellectual life in those who are thus spoken of, but from the fact that the intellectual part of them is so blended and lost in the rounded and symmetrical unity of their life that you have never been led to think of it by itself. All this is very frequently true concerning women, whose unity of life is often more apparent than is that of men.

Again, the superiority of this sort of life is seen in the instinctive way with which men seek to produce it in their systems of education for the young. In the family and in the school parents and teachers whose own ambitions are purely and hardly intellectual will rarely seek for children so narrow an existence as they are practically seeking for themselves. All men who have anything to do with education are drawn irresistibly into the valuing of character. They cannot disregard subjective life. They cannot sow seed over the fallow ground till they have first made it fertile with right emotion. And, on the other hand, the intellectual culture of the race, strong as the motives are that incite men to it for its own sake, could probably never maintain its ground and keep the enthusiastic interest of the best and wisest men if, in spite of countless disappointments, it were not clearly seen to live, upon the whole, a close connection with men's moral conditions and the symmetrical completeness of their lives.

But perhaps what I am urging is seen most clearly if we watch the change which comes to all our natures in their loftiest, which are their truest, moods. The best study of essential human nature is to be found, not in the exceptional men who stand out distinct above their fellows, nor in the ordinary man in his ordinary moments, when the fire of his life burns low, but in those states which come to all healthily susceptible human natures, in which their powers are most active with the least distortion, — times of exaltation, in which the exalted man is conscious that he is not transported out of himself, but is simply realizing himself in a supreme degree. And one of the characteristics of such times of healthy exaltation is the manifest unity of the life, and especially the way in which intellectual action, without being quenched, nay, burning at its very brightest, blends with the quickened activity of all the being, and is not even thought of by itself. A time of heroic sacrifice brings quick perceptions, which yet the hero has no time to dwell upon with pride before they are lost in the torrent of rich impulses which is sweeping through his life. The days when death comes near our life with that freedom and refinement which it always tries to bring, are days in which we think the truest and profoundest thoughts about the overpowering mystery; but it is so much else to us then besides a thing to think about,— it is something so much nearer and greater than a problem of the brain,— that we hardly know that we are thinking about it at all. So love and hope and joy and indignation and fervent admiration for a noble man, and any sudden sight of our own best possibilities,— all of these are conditions in which the intellect works vigorously, but it works in the midst of a being all quickened and exalted together, and so it is lost in the large action of the whole. " He who does not lose his reason in certain things," says Lessing, " has none to lose." But the reason is lost, not by any palsy or death that falls on it, but by the vehement life of will and affections, among which the life of the reason takes its true place as but one member of the perfect whole.

There is a noble passage of Wordsworth which tells this same story, and shows how under the greatest influences of nature the same rich blending of the life takes place. He is describing the consecrating effects of early dawn : —

> " What soul was his when from the naked top
> Of some bold headland he beheld the sun
> Rise up and bathe the world in light. He looked —
> Ocean and earth, the solid frame of earth
> And ocean's liquid mass, beneath him lay
> In gladness and deep joy. The clouds were touched,
> And in their silent faces did he read
> Unutterable love. Sound needed not
> Nor any voice of joy: his spirit drank
> The spectacle; sensation, soul, and form
> All melted into him. They swallowed up
> His animal being; in them did he live
> And by them did he live. They were his life.
> In such access of mind, in such high hour
> Of visitation from the Living God,
> Thought was not; in enjoyment it expired.
> No thanks he breathed, he proffered no request;
> Rapt into still communion that transcends
> The imperfect offices of prayer and praise,
> His mind was a thanksgiving to the Power
> That made him; it was blessedness and love!"

I must not dwell longer on these illustrations. This fact, so abundantly set forth in our own best experiences, is the fact that fills and ex-

plains the intellectual history of Jesus. The
"mind of Christ," of which one of His followers
spoke years afterwards, is mingled and lost in
the completeness of His life ; and that completeness, to take one step farther, is represented
to Himself by the obedience which He owed
and always rendered to His Father. The unity
of life is rescued from vagueness and made a true
reality to Jesus by the one enveloping relation
to God which comprehends it all. We shall understand that, I think, if we turn again to the
unique and precious story in which is told us all
that we know about the boyhood of Jesus. The
child of twelve years old finds his way back to
the Temple, where the sacredness of life and
the connection of man with God had for the
first time been set forth before Him in ceremo-
nial richness. He cannot turn His back upon
the wonderful, delightful place. He cannot go
quietly down into Galilee, and leave the Temple,
which is radiant with knowledge and holiness,
behind Him. We must remember that the
Temple was indeed the centre of knowledge for
the Jews. There sat the doctors. There the

law was taught. When Jesus, then, tarried in Jerusalem and clung about the Temple courts, it was the craving after knowledge, it was that sweet, vague outlook into vast cloud-swept fields of possible intelligence, which makes the poetry of every pure boy's life to-day, — it was this lofty wish to know, that kept Him there. But when His parents came back and found Him, and when, with a boy's directness and a boy's absorption in the present task, He looked up at them in surprise, as if it were a wonderful thing that any one should think He could be doing anything but just what He was doing then, and answered, "Wist ye not that I must be about My Father's business?" it was an answer of obedience; all alive with thought; yet, when He stated the purpose of His life, it was not thought, but duty. The intellectual activity was held in the bosom of an obedience which made the boy's life a unit. Out of that obedience the intellectual activity received its impulse, and to the more and more complete fulfilment of that obedience it contributed its results.

Thus the character of the intellectual life of

Jesus was indicated at the very start. We have only to look at some of the striking moments of His mental experience, to see how that character ran through them all. There is much that might be said about the Temptation, — that mysterious experience in the wilderness with which His early life of contemplation passed over into the later life of action. All that I point out to you now is this, — that, while it is evident that in those terrible hours the whole nature of Jesus was submitted to a fearful struggle, and that, as not the least among the elements that made up the ordeal, His intellectual judgments were shaken, His knowledge of truth was invaded by tumultuous doubt, His sight of His Father was obscured, — yet, at the last, and as the sum of all, the question was not one of intelligence but of will. It was a choice of obediences that made the real crisis. It was the rejection of Satan's "Fall down and worship me," and the clear acceptance of "Thou shalt serve the Lord Thy God," that marked the victory. "Then the Devil leaveth Him, and behold angels came and ministered unto Him." The moment that the obedience of the life was established, the mental tumult settled into peace within it.

At the other end of the career of Jesus the same thing was seen. In the Garden of Gethsemane reason seemed to totter on her throne. For the last time the desperate hands had to cling to the truth in instant fear. But there, too, it is not by the direct conviction of the reason; it is by the adjustment of the whole life in obedience — to which, no doubt, the reason gave its assent, but which was a transaction far beyond the reason's limits — that the trembling reason finds composure. When He said, "Thy will be done," all the obscurity began to scatter, and those words which He said four days later, after He had risen, to His disciples, "Ought not Christ to have suffered these things?" — words with the echo in them of the same surprise with which He long before spoke to His parents in the Temple, — words full of the peace of satisfied intelligence, — began to take shape upon His lips.

It is a poor and pitiable life indeed that cannot understand in some degree, out of its own history, this experience of the Temptation and of Gethsemane. Who of us has not bowed his will to some supreme law, accepted some obedience as the atmosphere in which his life must live, and found at once that his mind's darkness turned to light, and that many a hard question found its answer? Who has not sometimes seemed to see it all as clear as daylight, that not by the sharpening of the intellect to super natural acuteness, but by the submission of the nature to its true authority, man was at last to conquer truth; that not by agonizing struggles over contradictory evidence, but by the harmony with Him in whom the answers to all our doubts are folded, a harmony with Him brought by obedience to Him, our doubts must be enlightened?

But to return to Jesus, I think we have in what we have been saying the best light that we can get upon the method of His inspiration by His Father, and so, by inference, upon the method of all the inspiration of the holy men who spoke for God. When I hear Jesus say, "As My Father hath taught Me I speak these things; and He that sent Me is with Me: the Father hath not left Me alone; for I do always those things that please Him," I cannot be surprised as I read on to the next verse and find that "As He spake those words many believed on Him." For the words made the breadth and depth of His inspiration plain. At the base of it all lay His obedience: "For I do always those things that please Him." Out of that obedience came continual communion. "He that sent Me is with Me. The Father hath not left Me alone." And to the spirit lying close in that communion to the Father's spirit, to the soul of the Son lying in its completeness on the soul of the Father, came the wisdom of the Father to be given to the world. What did they think of the next truth that Jesus uttered after He had thus explained Himself? Did it seem to them something which He by unusual penetration had discovered? Did it seem to them a single, separate message, apart from all other communication, told by God to Jesus to be told to them? They must have understood Him better than that. They must have known that, however the intelligence of Jesus had been illuminated to know this special truth, that special illumination of the intelligence was subordinate to and included in the consecration of the whole life by obedience; that in whatever sense Jesus knew this because God told Him, He never could have been told if underneath all the communication between Him and His Father it had not been true at the base of everything that He and His Father were one. I cannot conceive of the true hearer of Jesus losing that large thought of His Lord's inspiration ever again. Not a mere message-bringer could He ever seem; but the eternal truth manifest first in character before it presented itself in specific revelation; the Word of God, in which and by which the words of God through Him gained their authority and value.

Once or twice Jesus declares with perfect frankness the limits of His knowledge. There are some things which He does not know. "Of that day and hour knoweth not the Son," He says, "but the Father." What does it mean? The ancient oracle or the modern fortune-teller could not do that and yet keep men's faith.

They have no self, no character behind their words. Men do not believe properly in them, but only in their words. But Jesus always is behind His words. "Ye believe not," He said once to the Jews, "because ye are not of My sheep." *He* must possess men before His words could take possession of them. We must believe Him inspired, see Him full of God, before we can believe His words inspired, and see them burn with truth. Not from simple brain to simple brain, as the reasoning of Euclid comes to its students, but from total character to total character, comes the New Testament from God to men.

If we turn now from the thought of Christ's own intellectual life to think of the immediate influence which He exercised upon His disciples, I do not know how to approach that part of our subject better than through the medium of an analogy which must be suggested to any one who thoughtfully reads the record of Jesus along with the record of that only one among purely human teachers whom Christian men have ever ventured to compare with Him. No one can read the Gospel of St. John and then turn to what is left us of the life of Socrates, without being struck and almost startled with the suggested comparison between the account of Christ's last talk with His disciples before His crucifixion, which is given in five chapters of that Gospel, and the beautiful story of what Socrates said to Simmias and Cebes and his other friends in the prison at Athens just before he drank the hemlock, - - the story which Plato has written for us in the Phædo. And nowhere could the essential difference as well as the likeness of the two great teachers become more apparent. Nowhere could the critics who loosely class Jesus and Socrates together see more distinctly where their classification fails, where the line runs beyond which Socrates cannot go, beyond which the nature of Jesus sweeps out of our sight.

I should like to dwell for a few moments on this comparison. The story in St. John is familiar enough. The points in the story which Plato tells I may venture to recall to you. The two may stand in our imagination side by side. And in their mere details there is much that suggests comparison. The quiet upper chamber at Jerusalem where the young man sits with His young companions at the simple supper, where venerable traditions blend with the joy of present companionship and the pain of coming separation, is set off against the rugged prison opening upon the Agora at Athens, where, in the inner chamber, the friends of Socrates have come to talk with him once more before he dies. The old man sits on the bed at first, with his leg drawn up, rubbing the spot from which the fetter had just been taken off preparatory to his death. The relief that he feels in his leg opens his talk with a remark upon the strange connection between pain and pleasure. By and by he drops his feet upon the floor, and so sits on the bedside, calmly talking. Once he drops his hand affectionately upon the head of Phædo, as if he, too, would have a "disciple whom he loved," and draw one trusting heart closer to him than the rest. His wife comes in to him with their three boys, and he talks with them kindly, but there is no tenderness, and after a little while he bids them to be taken away, for they evidently trouble him. The humor that had played through all his life is with him to the last. Once he makes a pun. And at the very end, when the disciples asked him how they should bury him, he bids them bury him what way they will, "if only you can catch me and I do not give you the slip"; and as he speaks, he gently smiles to see how lightly all that he has been saying has sunk into them, and to fancy these clumsy affectionate Athenians chasing his fleeting spirit to cage it in a tomb. Once comes a message from the executioner to tell him about the poison he will have to drink, which is a sharp, violent note, intruding on the music of his thought, that somehow reminds us of the departure of Judas from the Passover table. For an instant the coming woe starts up dramatically real. There is one beautiful moment when the disciples are half convinced, but still frightened and trembling. Socrates sees it in their faces, and tells them of it. And Cebes answers, "Well, Socrates, suppose that we are frightened; do you encourage and comfort us. Or rather, suppose not that we are frightened, but that there is a child within us who is so." And Socrates playfully takes up the pretty thought. "Ah, yes," he says, "we must find some charm that we can sing over this frightened child to quiet him," and so he goes on with his talk again. The words in which Phædo afterwards recalls the impression that his master's presence made on him that day might almost have been on the lips of John. "I had no painful feeling of pity, as might seem natural to a person present at such a catastrophe, nor did I feel a pleasure as on ordinary occasions when we talked philosophy, though the discourse was of the same kind. It was a peculiar feeling that possessed me, a strange mixture of pleasure and grief, when I thought that he would soon cease to be." All through the conversation we can hear the religious festival in which the Athenians are engaged outside, to celebrate the return of the sacred ship from Delos, — the Passover, as it were, of the Athenian life. At last, without a shock, continuing the calm and peaceful teaching to the last, the great man takes the cup and drinks the poison, and all is over

There lies his body before them, more eloquent in silence than any of the words he said.

And now what was it that they talked about on that last day? The discussion hovered and fluttered a little at first before it settled to its work; but it soon became a sustained argument for immortality. It is very hard to think that this man is just going to die, and knows it, who sits here calmly arguing that the soul must be immortal. And what were his arguments? Really, they were three. The first was the distinctness between the soul and the body, as testified by what was the favorite doctrine of Socrates, — the soul's pre-existence. If the soul existed before the body, it surely might outlive it. Nay, it must be ready for the other bodies which are waiting for it. In support of this belief he dwells upon his theory of recollection to account for the presence of ideas in man which man never could have acquired by the senses. Then comes his second argument, in which he pleads the indestructibility of the soul from its simplicity, its incomposite nature. Then Simmias and Cebes interpose two exquisitely stated difficulties; one suggesting that, after all, the soul may be to the body what the music is to the lyre; the other wondering whether the body may not possibly outlive the soul, as the unthinking cloth outlives the wise and skilful weaver by whose hand it was made. Socrates replies to both of them and satisfies them; and then goes on to his third argument, which is a long and very subtle one about ideas and their accessory attributes, in which he tries to draw the distinction between the imperishable idea and the perishable attributes of life.

These are his arguments. They are surrounded with an atmosphere of feeling. Reverence and gratitude to God, affection for his disciples, and a tender sense of duty, — these play around and through the whole discussion and give it softness and richness. It is not hard and cold. It does not rely wholly upon the worth of its arguments for its power. That is seen in the fact that, though the arguments in the shape in which Socrates puts them would convince no man of the truth of immortality to-day, still the whole scene remains as one of the sacred pictures of the human soul. That prison cell is one of the temples of man's faith, one of the vestibules of immortality. But still the discourse is an argument. It is a search after knowledge. It is a struggle of the intellect. It is consoled by the thought of a divinity behind it which will make allowance for its deficiencies; but it feels no direct and present influence from the wisdom of that divinity. What it knows it must discover for itself, and hold, when it is won, as an intellectual conviction. Now turn the leaves of four hundred years, and in the chamber of the Passover feel the difference. As Jesus speaks, argument disappears. Conviction is attained by the immediate perception of life by life. "If ye had known Me, ye should have known My Father also, and from henceforth ye both know Him and have seen Him." "In My Father's house are many mansions: I go to prepare a place for you." That is the argument of Jesus for immortality. It is not right to say that Socrates appeals to the reason and fails, while Jesus speaks to the heart and succeeds. The appeal of Jesus is to the reason, too, only it is to that spiritual reason which is no special function of the nature, but is the best action of the whole nature working together, the affection and the will being the partners of the brain; or rather, for that does not express the intimacy of their life, the affection and the will being one manhood with the brain and sharing its intelligence. The difference of result is, in one word, the difference between convincing the intellect and making the man believe.

I do not know that I can make this clearer, and I must not steal the time to quote largely from the discourse of Jesus in support of what I mean. But let us put one or two pairs of passages together. The philosopher asks, "Shall a man who really loves knowledge, and who is firmly persuaded that he shall never truly attain it except in Hades, be angry and sorry to have to die?" The Son of God says, "Now I go to Him that sent Me." Socrates says, "Be well assured I do expect this, that I shall be among good men, though this I do not feel so confident about; but I shall go to gods who are good governors" Jesus cries, "Now, O Father, glorify thou Me with Thine own self." Socrates draws in confused but elaborate detail the road to Hades and its geography. Jesus says, " In My Father's house are many mansions "; and, " Father, I will that they whom Thou hast given Me be with Me where I am." Socrates is noble in his frank uncertainty about his life. " Whether I tried in the right way and with what success I shall know certainly when I arrive there, if it please God." Jesus is divine in His certainty. " O righteous Father, the world hath not known Thee, but I have known Thee." " I have finished the work which Thou gavest Me to do." Socrates tells of a "demon," or angel, who has the care of every man while he is alive, and when he is dead takes him to the place of judgment. Jesus says, " I will pray the Father, and He shall give you another Comforter, that He may abide with you forever." " He shall testify of Me." The sage consoles his disciples by sending them out to find other teachers. "Greece is a wide place, Cebes, and there are in it many good men. And there are, besides, many races of barbarians, all of whom are to be explored in search of some who can perform such a charm as we have spoken of." The Savior declares simply, "I will not leave you comfortless. I will come unto you." Socrates says, when they ask him for his last legacy, "If you take good care of yourselves, you will always gratify me and mine most." Jesus says, "This is My commandment, that ye love one another as I have loved you." And, if we let our eye run out beyond the times when both the tragedies — the tragedy of Athens and the tragedy of Jerusalem — were finished, and see what thoughts of the two sufferers were left behind them, we hear Phædo closing his long story with these words: "This was the end, Echecrates, of our friend: of all the men whom we have known, the best, the wisest, and the most just." Nay; before the poison was given by the jailer's hand we hear him say to his great prisoner, "I have found you the most generous and gentle and best of all who ever came here." And then our thoughts run to Jerusalem, and hear the centurion who commanded the soldiers who crucified Jesus say, as he sees the Crucified give up the ghost, "Truly this was the Son of God."

I know not what to say to any man who does not feel the difference. I can almost dream what Socrates would say to any man who said there was no difference between Jesus and him. But how shall we state the difference? One is divine and human; the other is human only. One is Redeemer; the other is philosopher. One is inspired, and the other questions. One reveals, and the other argues. These statements, doubtless, are all true. And in them all there is wrapped up this, which is the truth of all the influence of Jesus over men's minds, that where Socrates brings an argument to meet an objection, Jesus always brings a nature to meet a nature, — a whole being which the truth has filled with strength, to meet another whole being which error has filled with feebleness.

I must hasten on to speak of the special characteristics which this general character of His teaching gave to the influence which Jesus exercised over the intellectual life of His disciples. But let me ask you first to remember two notable utterances of His, in which He distinctly stated this theory of the mind and its work, which we have gathered by inference from many of His words. One of them is in those words which it would seem as if a great deal of the broadest and best religious thought of our age had almost taken for its motto. No doubt, like all mottoes, it has been often in danger of losing some of its profoundness by the very familiarity which it has gained, as a coin loses sharpness by the constant circulation which proves that men know its value; but, on the whole, I do not know what verse there is in the New Testament which any man who longed to see the intellect of men most alive and most thoroughly consecrated to the best uses, would sooner choose to write upon the walls of his thoughtful century than that which Jesus spoke in the Temple about the midst of the feast: "If any man will do My will, He shall know of the doctrine." The other passage is that beautiful account of the simple and humble wonder of Judas, not Iscariot, who found it hard to believe that he and his brother disciples were to receive enlightenments from God which did not come to other men. And

Jesus went on to explain the process to him. "If a man love Me," He said, "he will keep My words, and My Father will love him, and We will come to Him and make our abode with Him." Those, I think, are the two critical passages in which Jesus gives us His doctrine of the intellectual life. They are as clear and definite as if they were written in a book of science. They both declare that in the highest things the intellect can never work alone for the discovery of truth. Truth, when it is won, is the possession of the whole nature. By the action of the whole nature only can it be gained. The king must go with his counsellors at his side and his army at his back, or he makes no conquest. The intellect must be surrounded by the richness of the affections and backed by the power of the will, or it attains no perfect truth.

Of such an influence, what was the effect on those disciples? What sort of an intellectual life did they attain? It is not hard to point out some, at least, of the habits of mind into which Jesus led them. The first is their habit of regarding the physical world as the utterance of a divine will, in sympathy with the divine character. There are two ways of looking at the earth which have divided men in all time. The one has counted it something outside of man, with only external relation to him, holding him, feeding him, forcing him to work. The other has counted it in some true sense a medium of revelation and influence from God to man. The first view is the view of science, and is always tending to hard superficialness, to the spiritual poverty of the fingering slave who will " peep and botanize upon his mother's grave." The other view is the view of poetry, and its corrupt tendency is toward superstition, — toward that excessive human self-consciousness which thinks that stars move and winds blow only to bring us messages out of the unseen world. Between these two conceptions of nature all human thought divides. "Poetry," says Coleridge, "is not the proper antithesis to prose, but to science." Science looks to the world for facts and knowledge; poetry asks of it influence and character. Science handles the material; poetry questions the creative soul within. Each has its proper business with this wondrous earth. Each makes its admirable kind of man. Sometimes, though very rarely, the two meet in the same man; but never so that one or the other is not in clear preponderance and does not give a distinct color to the character. Now of the Apostles there can be no doubt which view of the earth their Lord had led them to. His parables, — the stories of the wheat and tares in the field, of the fig-tree on the hillside, of the sheep wandering in the mountains, of the net dragged through the rushing waters of the lake, — all of them were poems; all of them sought in nature not the form, but the soul, not the shape, but the meaning. And when the disciples wanted to call down the fire from heaven to destroy a village of the Samaritans where Jesus had not been received, it was the poetic thought of nature that was in their minds. Nothing could have been more unscientific. It was very crude and ignorant, — poor poetry, poor sense of the meaning of the natural forces, of the purpose of the heavens and their fire, and of the way in which their power could be shown, — but it was the crudeness of the poet, not of the scientist; it was the vague and coarse effort of that same power which, made clear and fine, enabled them to understand the parables of Jesus and not to be offended at His miracles, — which finally prepared them for the resurrection, and made St. Matthew not afraid to write that when Jesus expired on the cross the earth quaked, and the rocks rent, and the graves were opened.

To this same spirit it belonged to easily acknowledge mystery, or the largeness of life, its necessary extension into regions which they had not explored. Men are made quite as much by their sense of what there is in the world which they do not know, as by the few truths of which they think that they have gained the mastery. The outlook into mystery has even a stronger intellectual influence than the inspection of discovered fact. The sin with which Jesus was always upbraiding the Pharisees — what He called hypocrisy — is at once a spiritual and an intellectual vice. It was a disbelief of the greatness of God which made it possible for them to dream of imposing upon Him. It was a pride in them selves which could not look into the vastness of truth. The unbelief which Jesus upbraids is not the doubt of special doctrine, but that narrow and worldly temper to which the whole world of mystery was inconceivable. The doubter whom Christ rebukes is not the earnest and eager believer who has become lost in the highways of faith. It is the unventuresome spirit which is incapable of faith at all, which has reduced the world to materialism like the Sadducee, or made duty into law and religion into ceremony like the Pharisee. For neither of them was there any outlook. For His disciples, the word of intellectual life, as of moral discipline, was "Watch." "Expect new things. The world is large. Out of the darkness shall come light. Be ready for surprises." Such readiness is the rightful possession only of men who live not in the forms but in the principles of things; and so the spiritual thoroughness into which Jesus led His disciples is bound up closely with the intellectual progress which they attained.

Again, Jesus inspired them with His own view of the actual condition of things around them, and of the way in which the better life of the world was to come. The character of Christ's own reforming spirit was clear enough. He said that He wanted not to destroy, but to fulfil the agencies which He found here in the world. He never cared to reshape circumstances until He had regenerated men. He let the shell stand as He found it until the new life within could burst it for itself. It is very wonderful to me to see how thoroughly His disciples caught His method. They could not have caught it so completely and so soon if it had not been that it was based on a large principle, if it had not been more than a special trick or tact. Almost instantly, as soon as the disciples began their work, they seem to have been filled with a true conception of its divine method, — that not from outside, but from inside; not by the remodelling of institutions, but by the change of character; not by the suppression of vices, but by the destruction of sin, the world was to be saved. That truth with whose vitality all modern life has flourished, with the forgetfulness of which all modern history has always tended to corruption, that truth only dreamed of by a few spiritual philosophers in the ancient world, — it is one of the marvellous phenomena of human thought, that it should have leaped full-grown to life with the first influence of Christianity. A few faint flutterings about the old methods of repression, and the disciples of Jesus settle at once to the new methods of development.

Another of the intellectual habits which naturally grew out of the first principles of Jesus was His discovery of interest in people whom the world generally would have found most uninteresting. And this same habit, passing over into His disciples, made the wide and democratic character of the new faith. There are signs enough that Jesus had His special feelings towards these men who were most congenial to Him. As the most prominent of all such signs, we all remember His peculiar love for the perceptive and appreciative John. At the table of the Last Supper, by the cross from which the Sufferer looked down on His few faithful friends, on the morning of the resurrection, at the Sea of Tiberias, where the risen Jesus met the familiar company again, — everywhere John appears as the disciple whom Jesus loved. We cannot picture to ourselves a character so definite as that of Jesus which should be destitute of such affinities; and yet, always, as we read the Gospels, there is a larger fact behind this special friendship, — there is a value of human nature and of all men who bear it, on the bosom of which this special friendship floats like a mere accident. The result is, a true freedom from fastidiousness, a breadth and quickness of sympathy and hope which gives a singular largeness to the intellectual life of Jesus, which we all recognize. Something of the same sort begins to show itself at once in His disciples. I do not know how we better can describe it than by saying that it keeps all the warmth and directness of personal intercourse without its distortions and partialities. This is an intellectual as well as a spiritual condition. It keeps thought and observation large, and makes the judgment at once earnest and true. It is the power that redeems the mind from narrowness while it still keeps it eager and intense.

There is one other habit which characterized always the thought of Jesus, and which also passed out from Him to his disciples. It is not easy to describe, but it seems to consist in a constant progress from the arbitrary and special to the essential and universal forms of thought. In one part of the Sermon on the Mount this habit of Jesus is supremely manifest. It is told in the fifth chapter of St. Matthew. The Pharisees — those dull and earthly spirits who yet have drawn forth for us the divinest words of Jesus — had followed the great Teacher and were persecuting Him with questions. Those questions were all of the same sort. They all began with some special law, sometimes of the Old Testament, sometimes of the Rabbinical traditions, and went on to the inevitable conflict of that law in its letter with the conditions of human life. The law was good, but the mere letter of the law became exhausted or confused before it had accomplished the purpose for which the law was evidently made. Jesus takes each of these laws and opens it. Its principle appears underneath its letter. It is seen to be no arbitrary enactment for the settlement of a special difficulty, but an essential truth, true everywhere. For instance, the prohibition of murder opens into the picture of a vigorous and vital peace out of which all malice and hatred should have faded away. The prohibition of adultery enlarges itself into the picture of a world all bright with purity. The command to perform an oath expands into the promise of a life so simply pure and faithful that in it no oath should ever need be spoken. The "eye for an eye, and tooth for a tooth" changes into "resist not evil," and men see how all justice has mercy at its heart. There is nothing that marks the limits of men's intellectual life more than the degree in which they have the power of this progress from the local to the universal, from the partial to the complete. All thought, like all life, must begin with specialness, must fasten itself upon one point of the great earth; but just as Jesus in his influence upon our race has left behind Judea and its geography and gone forth to become the possession of the world, so it would seem as if His teaching were always starting from special problems only to extend itself to the great principles which underlie those problems and which have their applications throughout all human life.

Indeed, I think that the figure which I just suggested is one that may give us a good deal of light. I remember years ago how the first sight of Palestine seemed to adjust for me the two thoughts of the local and the universal Christ as I had never been able to adjust them before. As one travels through that land, the New Testament story is rescued from vagueness and obscurity, and the historic life becomes a clear and realized fact; while at the same time the poverty of the country, the failure of the material to satisfy and account for and accompany the spiritual, sets one free for a larger and truer grasping of the Divine power. It is like the relation between an immortal word and the mortal lips that uttered it. The lips die, and you look at them when they are dead, and see at once how they were made to speak the word, how their whole mechanism was built for it, and yet how, even while they uttered it, they were dying in giving expression to what by its very nature was eternal. So Palestine, the home-land of Jesus, opens into Christendom; and so each arbitrary command and special revelation which He gave opens into eternal principles and universal truths.

A poetic conception of the world we live in, a willing acceptance of mystery, an expectation of progress by development, an absence of fastidiousness that comes from a sense of the possibilities of all humanity, and a perpetual enlargement of thought from the arbitrary into the essential, — these, then, I think, are the intellectual characteristics which Christ's disciples gathered from their Master; and I think that we can see that these characteristics make, as we set them all together, a certain definite and recognizable type of mental life, one that we should know from every other if we met to-day a man in whom it was embodied. It is a type in which, according to the description which I tried to give, the intellect, while it is plentifully present, does not stand alone and force itself upon our thought It is a type in which character is the result that impresses us, — character holding in harmony all the elements of the nature, rather than intellect uality, which is the predominant presence of one element. It is a type in which righteousness and reason so coincide and co-operate that you cannot separate them, and do not want to. It is a type of life in which, fulfilling the conjunction which David loved so much to describe, " Mercy and Truth are met together."

If I have rightly traced the general character of the mental life and influence of Jesus, we are prepared now, I think, to bring it home into association with that which through all these lectures we have held to be the central and formative idea of Jesus. I have drawn the indications of His intellectual character from what is told us in the Gospel of John. One key-word, truth, appears, as I said, upon His lips, almost exclusively in that book. And now in that same book it is almost alone that Jesus is always calling God His Father. Mark does not quote at all such words, and Matthew and Luke quote them very seldom. The two, then, go together. That same profounder insight into the mind of Jesus which sees His intellectual life and influence not standing alone, but part of the whole nature, seizes also upon that representation which sums up His whole life as the life of a son lived in the household of his father. And we can see ourselves why this is so. As soon as we unite in our minds the various characteristics which we have seen to belong to the intellectuality of Jesus, and then look about the world for any picture of an intellectual life which shall present to us, however faintly, the total impression which they make, we find ourselves drawn at once to the learning child in His Father's house. The poetic conception of the world, the satisfied acceptance of mystery, the constant thought of development, the absence of fastidiousness, and the perpetual opening of the arbitrary into the essential,— all of these blend most healthily in that primary type of intellectual influence which is seen wherever a docile child stands learning truth within his father's house. It is no hard touch of intellect on intellect. It is a warm approach of life to life, in which it is not merely knowledge but character, in which knowledge is held in solution, that passes over from the wiser to the foolisher. If this be true, then see what we have reached.

Here at the bottom of His intellectual life and influence, as at the bottom of all His other life and influence, lies the idea of Jesus. Still before all things, at the root and source of everything else that He is, He is the Son of God. Once, when they would not understand Him, He turned sadly and looked forward past the crucifixion into the prospect of a fuller comprehension of it, which, it may be, we are only now beginning to attain ; and as He pictured it to his hope, this truth of His Sonship lay at the bottom of it. " When ye have lifted up the Son of Man," He said, " then shall ye know that I am He, and that I do nothing of Myself, but as My Father hath taught Me I speak these things." At the bottom of His whole conception of intellectual life lies the never-failing, never-fading consciousness that He is the child of God. You touch some flower of a parable, you are pierced by the sharp thorn of some rebuke, and when you ask for the secret of the sweetness or the pain you find it in the life-blood of this idea that comes up out of the deep heart of His life. You ask yourself what is the one quality that you must put into the wonderful talk of Socrates to make it approach the vastly more wonderful talk of Jesus, and you can name nothing but this, so wholly lacking in the sage of Athens, so totally pervading every word of the Man of Palestine, — the consciousness that He is God's child, knowing God as a son knows a father, speaking with an authority which no scribe can have, not because He knows more things, but because He knows everything differently in that ever-present sense of Sonship.

There is one short story in the Gospel of St. John, which, if we had the time to study it in detail, would teem with illustration of what I have been saying. It is the story of Nicodemus, — a very precious passage for the understanding of the intellectual method of Jesus. Nicodemus is one of St. John's men. Neither of the other writers is drawn to him. But St. John seems, as he writes the narrative, to feel that he is opening to us his Master's very heart. If we had time to dwell minutely on the story, we should see how Jesus does for Nicodemus the three things which every thorough teacher must do for every scholar. He gives him new ideas, He deepens with these ideas his personal character and responsibility, and He builds for him new relations with his fellow-men. When Nicodemus goes away from Jesus, he carries with him the new truth of regeneration; he is trembling with the sense that, to make that truth thoroughly his, he himself must be a better man; and by and by he is seen setting himself against the current of his fellow-judges to speak a word for the Master who had spoken such educating words to him. These are the elements that make up the effect of all effective influence, — new truth, new character, new duty, not distinct, not distinguishable from each other, but all mingled in one complete change and elevation of the man's whole nature. And when we look for the spring on which Christ laid His hand for such a comprehensive awakening of the man's life, we find it where we should have looked for it, in the truth of sonship brought to the world in Him, — "God so loved the world that He gave His only-begotten Son." There is an old legend which says that Nicodemus and Gamaliel and St. Stephen were buried close together, and that years afterwards their bodies were found side by side. In a certain way they belong together. They were all students of the things of God, various types of sacred wisdom. But if we want to rate them rightly, we shall find the fineness and the loftiness of their intellectual life to stand just in proportion to the fulness and clearness with which at the heart of each man's knowledge lay the idea of Jesus, that man is the son of God.

I want to spend what little time is yet left me in this lecture and this course in trying to trace the presence in all the intellectual life of Christendom of those peculiar characteristics, or rather of that peculiar character, which we have seen to-day to belong to the intellectual life of Jesus and His disciples. Christ's method of knowledge has been always present under the currents of modern thought and the impulses of modern study, and he who watches closely can see how they bear witness to its presence even while they are not conscious of it as they move upon its bosom. In one brief statement of it, the method of Jesus may be summed up thus: At the bottom of all truth lies the truth of truths, that man is the child of God. All that man knows is really a knowing of his Father, and can be thoroughly won only by obedience. And so the moral, the spiritual, and the intellectual lives are one.

The first consequence of the constant presence of this method is in a continual struggle after symmetry in the intellectual action of mankind. The tendency of modern times, often thwarted and defeated, is not to be thoroughly and finally content with one-sided development, with the use and development of certain special faculties of men. Sometimes this symmetry will be conceived of as something only to be attained by the race at large; others, more bold and idealistic, will dare to anticipate it even for the individual; but before all men who watch the human intellect there will hover a dream of the fulfilment of human life on every side, of the ultimate shaping of a symmetrical manhood in which the functions which seem contrary or independent shall be brought into absolute harmony and co-operation. Lacordaire writes of the "tortures of conscience struggling with genius." The highest Christian hope for man pictures the issue of that struggle in a lofty peace where both shall find their perfect satisfaction. Goldsmith, when he dedicates his comedy of "She Stoops to Conquer" to Dr. Johnson, says, "It may serve the interests of mankind, also, to inform them that the greatest wit may be found in a character without impairing the most affected piety." It may be doubted whether a somewhat finer wit and a somewhat loftier piety than the great London sage possessed must not be shown before the harmony of wit and piety shall be complete; but no man who is a Christian is willing to accept an impious wit or a witless piety as the final accomplishment of man, and all modern education, while it sometimes seems to attempt their union only by the rapid succession, and not by the harmonious mingling of the scientific and the moral instructions, acknowledges that both are necessary to the perfect man.

Again, the Christian thought of knowledge must always seek, not merely symmetry in the **knowing man**, but also harmony in all the knowledge he can win. Under one fatherhood the whole world becomes sacred. The old distinctions of useful and useless knowledge will not hold. The responsibility of each man for the working of his intellect must be acknowledged. The sin of mental carelessness or wilfulness must take its place among the sins against which men struggle and for which they repent. The application of moral standards to history, to art, and to pure letters must be learned and taught. The isolation of the artistic impulse from all moral judgments and purposes must be restrained and remedied. The whole thought of art must be enlarged and mellowed till it develops a relation to the spiritual and moral natures as well as to the senses of mankind. It will lose, perhaps, the purity and simplicity which has belonged to the idea of art in classic and unchristian times, but it will become more and more a part of the general culture of human life. That is the change which has come between the Venus of Milo and the Moses of Michael Angelo; between the Iliad and Paradise Lost; between the Idyls of Theocritus and the best modern novel. Mere simplicity of method and effect have given place to harmony of method and effect, littleness to largeness, fastidiousness to sympathy, and the Christian world has really learned more and more to believe what the Christian poet sang, that

> "He who feels contempt
> For any living thing, hath faculties
> That he hath never used: and Thought with him
> Is in its infancy."

Another truth which modern and Christian thought must make more and more of as it grows riper is the immediateness of divine influence. The ancient poet invoked his muse as he began his poem, but the invocation must have meant very little to him. It was the striking of the strings before he settled into the full strain he meant to play; as if he said to the world, "Listen, for I am ready with my song." The Christian thinker summons no muse, but as he speaks there is a sense of something vast behind him out of which influences come to him; there is conviction which is not born out of mere self-conceit; there is earnestness which is not the self-excitement of the Pythian damsel on her tripod. There is in all men who command the ears of other men a sense of something behind them — some call it truth, some call it God — for which, for whom, they speak. This is the loftier tone in modern speculation. This is the feminine element in modern thought, perpetually inspiring and leading and lifting that masculine reason,

> "Whose halting wisdom after knows
> What her diviner virtue fore discerns."

The intellectual life of Christendom, again, tends to democracy. Less and less will it consent to be the privilege of the selected few. The fact is plain. The reason of the fact is no less clear to one who traces the idea of Jesus everywhere. It is impossible to keep the bounds of mental life shut against any man when the source of all men's knowledge is in God, who is the Father of us all, and when the faculty of knowledge is closely connected with the faculty of moral obedience, which is the right and duty of mankind. Instantly this began when Christianity was once a living fact. Peter stepped out of the chamber of the Pentecost and spoke to the great multitude in words which assumed in them the power of understanding, of judging, of deciding questions which up to that time had been the sacred possession of the scribes and doctors. There was nothing like that speech before that day. The germs of the modern sermon, the modern lecture, and the modern school were in it. Thenceforth men's intellects might differ, but the intellectual chance was open to every man. To the dullest child belonged the right to learn all that he could learn, all that it was in him to learn, of His Father.

And yet once more. The everlasting progress of knowledge was assured. Once stretch an infinite life behind our human lives, on which they rest, in which they belong, and how the everlasting contradiction between the little that we know already, and the vast uncertain bulk of what we do not know, is robbed of its oppressiveness. There are two classes of men, with two dispositions, which come from that contradiction. One man, frightened at the great bulk of ignorance, refuses to look it in the face, flees for the preservation of his self-content to the little that he knows, makes believe that that is all there is to know, and refuses to hear of any more. He is the bigot who lives through all the ages and is found in every climate of the globe and every region of human study. Another man is so fascinated by the unknown that he refuses to place value on the known. The little which man has gained amounts to nothing. And with the depreciation of all present knowledge comes the loss of any solid starting-point for advance into the great vague world that lies beyond. He is the sceptic who mocks the bigot for his obstructiveness, and yet himself makes no progress because he has no foothold from which he can move. It is like the vague air taunting the solid rock. If in our modern Christian times there is a better spirit than either of these men can show; if it is not necessary for us that we should be bigots or sceptics either; if it is possible for us to value every fragment of knowledge, not for itself alone, but for the whole, of which it is a part, and which it prophecies and promises; if, as we gaze into the darkness of the unknown we are not paralyzed, but inspired, because in what we know already we hold the clew which, as it runs out into the darkness, we can feel fastened at the other end to the throne around which burns the unapproachable light of perfect knowledge toward which we may freely and eternally advance, — the reason of it all must be that the idea of Jesus has bound our ignorance and the knowledge of God together, and made it possible for man so to count all that his Father knows as the great region for his soul to grow in, and so to value the little he knows as the gift and pledge and promise of his Father, who knows all, that he can neither be proud of his own wisdom nor be dismayed before his own ignorance; but must live, as the child lives in his father's house, the happy life of complete humility and unlimited hope.

I must not linger at the close. If in these lectures I have failed to show that which it has been upon my mind and heart to describe, I shall not in a few last words redeem my failure.

I dare not, I do not hope that I have succeeded; but I hope that I have not wholly failed. For to me what I have tried to say is more and more the glory and the richness and the sweetness of all life. The idea of Jesus is the illumination and the inspiration of existence. Without it moral life becomes a barren expediency, and social life a hollow shell, and emotional life a meaningless excitement, and intellectual life an idle play or stupid drudgery. Without it the world is a puzzle, and death a horror, and eternity a blank. More and more it shines the only hope of what without it is all darkness. More and more the wild, sad, frightened cries of men who believe nothing, and the calm, earnest, patient prayers of men who believe so much that they long for perfect faith, seem to blend into the great appeal which Philip of Bethsaida made to Jesus at that Last Supper, where so much of our time in these four hours has been spent, — " Lord, show us the Father, and it sufficeth us." And more and more the only answer to that appeal seems to come from the same blessed lips that answered Philip, the lips of the Mediator Jesus, who replies, " Have I been so long with you and yet hast thou not known Me? He that hath seen Me hath seen the Father."

A VALUABLE SERIES OF SERMONS.

PREACHERS OF THE AGE.

The volumes are uniform in size, appearance and price, and each contains some twelve or fourteen Sermons or Addresses specially chosen or written for the series. They are issued in 12mo size, cloth extra, at **$1.25** each, and contain fine **Photogravure Portraits** reproduced, in most instances, from **unpublished** photographs.

"An excellent series."—*N. Y. Evangelist.*

1 **Living Theology.**
By EDWARD WHITE BENSON, D.D., Archbishop of Canterbury. 13 Sermons, 236 pages. Portrait. $1.25.
"Dr. Benson displays three traits at once—elegant and critical scholarship, philosophic thought, and deep spirituality."
—*Christian Union.*

2 **The Conquering Christ,**
And Other Sermons. By ALEXANDER MACLAREN, D.D. 14 Sermons, 212 pages. Portrait. $1.25.
"Dr. Maclaren has no superior, perhaps no equal, in the British pulpit in the analysis of Scripture in his deep searching for the hidden riches on which he is to build."—*Independent.*

3 **Verbum Crucis.**
Being Ten Sermons on the Mystery and the Words of the Cross. To which are added some other sermons preached on public occasions. By WILLIAM ALEXANDER, D.D., Bishop of Derry and Raphoe. 14 Sermons, 206 pages. Portrait. $1.25.
"These addresses on the seven sayings will be found very useful for those clergy who wish to give their people on Good Friday a service of devotion, and yet are too crowded with work to prepare their own material."—*Churchman.*

E. P. DUTTON & CO., PUBLISHERS, NEW YORK.

4 **Ethical Christianity.**
A Series of Sermons by HUGH PRICE HUGHES, M.A., of the West End Wesleyan Mission. 14 Sermons, 190 pages. Portrait. $1.25.
" We are convinced that there is no American minister who will not be wonderfully stimulated by reading these fourteen discourses. . . . . He has got a message from his heart, and he tells it in simple, tender, straight, heart language."—*Zion's Herald.*

5 **The Knowledge of God,**
And Other Sermons. By WILLIAM WALSHAM HOW, D.D., Bishop of Wakefield. 17 Sermons, 220 pages. Portrait. $1.25.
" Marked not only by the Bishop's well-known power of putting difficult truths into ' plain words,' but by that loving and persuasive spirit which gives him his great charm as a preacher."
—*London Guardian.*

6 **Light and Peace.**
Sermons and Addresses. By HENRY ROBERT REYNOLDS, D.D. 13 Sermons, 224 pages. Portrait. $1.25.
" Dr. Reynolds belongs by long possessed rights in this series. He is an English Congregationalist, since 1860 Principal of Lady Huntingdon's College, Cheshunt, Herts. He has been prolific with his pen in many directions. The sermons in this collection are elevated in theme and treatment. They touch the noblest themes in a noble manner, and with much imaginative power and eloquent force."—*Independent.*

7 **The Journey of Life.**
By W. J. KNOX LITTLE, M.A. 11 Sermons, 226 pages. Portrait. $1.25.
" The friends and admirers of the Rev. W. J. Knox Little, Canon of Worcester, will welcome this collection of clever sermons from him. The sermons all bear on some phase of the solemn thought suggested in the title, and bring up practical points which Canon Little knows well how to handle in a direct, wise and helpful manner."—*Independent.*

8 **Messages to the Multitude.**
By C. H. SPURGEON. 12 Sermons, 318 pages. Portrait. $1.25.
" This volume shows the great preacher at his best in the treatment of the Divine Word, and it will be, with the lifelike portrait of the preacher, a valuable memorial to the multitudes of his admirers."
—*N. Y. Observer.*

E. P. DUTTON & CO., PUBLISHERS, NEW YORK.

9 **Christ is All.**
Sermons from New Testament Texts, on various Aspects of the Glory and Work of Christ, with some Other Sermons. By H. C. G. MOULE, M.A., Principal of Ridley Hall, Cambridge, England. 18 Sermons, 248 pages. Portrait. $1.25.
"Devout and thoughtful expositions which cannot fail to be helpful."—*Interior.*
"They breathe the very spirit and power of the Gospel."
—*Church Bells.*

10 **Plain Words on Great Themes.**
By J. OSWALD DYKES, D.D., Principal of the Theo. College of the Presbyterian Church of England. 15 Sermons, 224 pages. Portrait. $1.25.
"These discourses are full of freshness, spirituality and genuine power. Young preachers especially might study with peculiar profit the chief characteristics of these sermons. We can hardly recommend too strongly."—*Advance.*

11 **Children of God,**
And Other Sermons. By the Rev. E. A. STUART, Vicar of St. James's. Holloway. 20 Sermons, 246 pages. Portrait. $1.25.
"A collection of brilliant, dramatic and effective sermons by one of the rising preachers in the English Established Church."
—*Independent.*

12 **Christ in the Centuries,**
And Other Sermons. By A. M. FAIRBAIRN, D.D., Principal of Mansfield College, Oxford. 13 Sermons, 232 pages. Portrait. $1.25.
"They are fresh and striking in thought, noticeably choice in diction, and instinct with the wisdom of human experience and the spirituality which is the fruit of close and tender fellowship with Christ. . . . No man in England to-day is more thoroughly representative of English Congregationalism than he."
—*Congregationalist.*

13 **Agoniæ Christi.**
Being Sermons on the Sufferings of Christ, together with Others on His Nature and His Work. By WILLIAM LEFROY, D.D., Dean of Norwich. 11 Sermons, 234 pages. Portrait. $1.25.
"Eleven thoughtful, solemn, often profoundly tender and always deeply impressive sermons on the deity, humanity and sufferings of Jesus."—*Congregationalist.*

14 **The Transfigured Sackcloth,**
    And Other Sermons. By the Rev. W. L. WATKINSON.
    12 Sermons, 248 pages. Portrait. $1.25.

"The author is a Wesleyan minister of recognized eminence."

"Their central thought is strikingly embodied in the title of the volume. Man must perforce wear his sackcloth of suffering and failure in this life, but, to those who recognize the Father's hand, it becomes transfigured, a garb of glory and one of God's choicest blessings. We heartily commend the volume to our readers."
—*Living Church.*

15 **The Gospel of Work.**
    Sermons by ANTHONY W. THOROLD, D.D., Bishop of Winchester. 14 Sermons, 194 pages. Portrait. $1.25.

"His Book of Sermons will be highly appreciated by clergymen and laymen. Many another preacher can study these models of force, of grace and of rhetorical finish with great profit to himself and to his congregation."—*Watchman.*

16 **Vision and Duty.**
    A Series of Discourses. By the Rev. CHARLES A. BERRY, Minister of Congregational Church, Wolverhampton. 12 Sermons, 242 pages. Portrait. $1.25.

"Mr. Berry is entitled to a place among the foremost of the 'Preachers of the Age Series.' His sermons show richness of thought. His style is clear and resonant. In single sentences he drives home great truths. His presentation of these is masterful and could not fail to impress and inspire. Many of his utterances are thrilling."—*N. Y. Observer.*

17 **The Burning Bush,**
    And Other Sermons. By W. BOYD CARPENTER, D.D., Bishop of Ripon. 11 Sermons, 190 pp. Portrait. $1.25.

"We think this volume is the best in the whole of this good series (Preachers of the Age). The eleven sermons are some of the grandest sermons we have ever read. Bishop Boyd Carpenter's sermons always charm one when they can be listened to, but they have also the far rarer power of mightily influencing the reader when they appear in print."—*Church Bells.*

18 **The "Good Cheer" of Jesus Christ.**
    Sermons. By the Rev. CHARLES MOINET, M.A., St. John's Presbyterian Church, Kensington. 12 Sermons, 200 pages. Portrait. $1.25.

"These discourses are full of the milk and meat of the Word of God. They are rich in practical and sound teaching. They reveal the thinking of a man versed in theological knowledge, yet in touch with the needs of living men and able to speak to them words in season."—*N. Y. Observer.*

PHILLIPS BROOKS'S WRITINGS.

SERMONS. Five Volumes. 12mo, cloth, $1.75 ea.; paper, 50c ea.
—— Sermons. Vol. I. 25th Thousand.
—— Candle of the Lord and Other Sermons. Vol. II. 18th Thousand.
—— Sermons Preached in English Churches. Vol. III. 10th Thousand.
—— Twenty Sermons. Vol. IV. 10th Thousand.
—— The Light of the World and Other Sermons. Vol. V. 10th Thousand.
Tolerance. Two Lectures addressed to the Students of Several of the Divinity Schools of the Prot. Epis. Church. 16mo, 111 pages, paper, 50c; cloth, 75c.
Influence of Jesus. The Bohlen Lectures for 1879. 14th Thousand. 16mo, cloth only, $1.25.
Lectures on Preaching, delivered before the Divinity School of Yale College in January and February, 1877. 12th Thousand. 16mo, cloth only, $1.50.
A Christmas Sermon. Paper, 25c.
An Easter Sermon. Paper, 25c.
Symmetry of Life. An Address to Young Men. Paper, 25c.
The Good Wine at the Feast's End. A Sermon on the Gains of Growing Old. Paper, 25c.

BEAUTIFULLY ILLUSTRATED CAROLS, BY BISHOP BROOKS.

Phillips Brooks's Poems. 1 vol., beautifully illustrated. Cloth, $3.00.
Christmas Once is Christmas Still. A Christmas Carol. Illustrated. $1.00.
The Voice of the Christ Child. A Christmas Poem. Illustrated. $1.00.
O ! Little Town of Bethlehem. A Christmas Carol. Illustrated. 25c.
A Constant Christmas. Illustrated. $1.00.
Easter Angels. Illustrated. $1.00.
An Easter Carol—Tomb, Thou Shalt Not Hold Him Longer. Illustrated. 50c.
Tract on Baptism and Confirmation. 10c.

These books are for sale by all booksellers, or will be sent by mail, postpaid, on receipt of price by the publishers.

E. P. DUTTON & CO.,
31 West 23d St., New York.

www.ingramcontent.com/pod-product-compliance
Lightning Source LLC
Chambersburg PA
CBHW031937230426
43672CB00010B/1948